Getting Started in
Home-based
Childcare

rs and nannies

Sue Griffin

www.heinemann.co.uk
✓ Free online support
✓ Useful weblinks
✓ 24 hour online ordering

01865 888058

Heinemann
Inspiring generations

Heinemann Educational Publishers
Halley Court, Jordan Hill, Oxford OX2 8EJ
Part of Harcourt Ltd

Heinemann is the registered trademark of Harcourt Education Limited

First published 2006

10 09 08 07 06
10 9 8 7 6 5 4 3 2 1

British Library Cataloguing in Publication Data is available
from the British Library on request.

10-digit ISBN: 0 435402129
13-digit ISBN: 978 0 435402 12 9

Designed by GD Associates, Banbury
Typeset and illustrated by Tek-Art, Croydon, Surrey, UK
Original illustrations © Harcourt Education Limited, 2006
Cover design by Wooden Ark Studio
Printed in the UK by Bath Press
Cover photo © SuperStock
Picture research by Kath Kollberg

Acknowledgements
Every effort has been made to contact copyright holders of material reproduced in this book. Any
omissions will be rectified in subsequent printings if notice is given to the publishers.

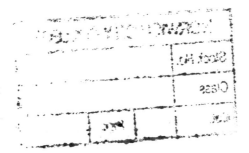

Contents

Acknowledgements

The author and publisher would like to thank NCMA for permission to reproduce covers of the following publications:

NCMA Accounts Book
NCMA childminder members' handbooks
NCMA nanny members' handbooks
Choosing a Home Childcarer
Employing an Approved Childcarer
NCMA Child Record Forms
NCMA Quality First Portfolio

Picture acknowledgements

The authors and publisher would like to thank the following individuals and organisations for permission to reproduce photographs:

Harcourt Education Ltd/Jules Selmes pp**vi**, **13**, **5**, **24**, **49**, **73**, **93**; Harcourt Education Ltd/Gareth Boden pp**11**, **16**, **27**, **38**, **51**, **59**, **81**, **82**, **87**, **88**, **100**, **104**, **122**, **128**, **130**; Harcourt Education Ltd/Tudor Photography pp**19**, **46**, **85**, **117**; Harcourt Education Ltd/Martin Sookias pp**135**; Getty Images/PhotoDisc pp**1**, **9**, **35**, **56**, **72**, **115**; Eyewire pp**89**, **137**; Corbis pp**101**; NCMA pp**140** left and right, **146**; Photolibrary pp**41**; Bubbles/Frans Rombout pp**112**; iStockPhoto/Jamie Wilson pp**120**; Digital Vision pp**55**; Alamy Images/Bananastock pp**69**.

Foreword

Welcome to this book, which, whether you are just starting out as a childminder or as a nanny, will give you plenty to think about. The book has background information, practical examples based on real life, and suggestions as to the decisions you'll need to make as part of your new career. It is also a useful companion to the *Introduction to Childcare Practice* (home-based) course.

In this book you will find information on topics such as: the ins and outs of registration and approval; the importance of children's learning; the impact your new career will have on you and your family; the business side of looking after children for a living; and keeping children safe and sound.

Home-based childcare is a valued and rewarding profession, and at the National Childminding Association we do everything we can to support you in your chosen career. For members we have: insurance packages; publications, including a regular magazine; telephone helplines; and training courses tailored to suit your needs.

Reading or studying this book is only one of the first steps you will take on your home-based childcarer journey – best wishes for a long and fulfilling career.

Charles Rice
Director of Children's Workforce Development
National Childminding Association (NCMA)

About the author

Sue Griffin has been involved in the early years and childcare field for over 25 years. She worked for 18 years for NCMA – in latter years as National Training and Quality Assurance Manager, developing the first national qualification and quality assurance schemes for childminders.

Sue was also a member of the Under Sevens Project team in 1989/90 which developed the first NVQs. She was involved in the playgroup movement in the 1980s and was national chair of the Preschool Playgroup Association (PPA).

She is now 'semi-retired' and works as a freelance consultant and writer for a wide range of organisations: National Children's Bureau, The Open University, Home-Start, CACHE, National Extension College, Practical Professional Childcare and NCMA.

Sue is a magistrate and sits on the family panel. She is also a member of the Early Education Advisory Group of the Sure Start Unit at the DfES and a trustee of the National Toy and Leisure Libraries Association. She enjoys being a Granny.

This book is dedicated to Rod, with love.

Introduction

Who is this book for?

This book is for people who have made the decision to work with children in a home-based setting, rather than in a group or centre-base, as:

- a registered childminder
- an approved nanny
- an approved over-sevens childminder.

Working with children is one of the most valuable jobs in society. You can be sure of job satisfaction, knowing that you are playing a key role in ensuring children's well-being and helping their development, by working closely with their families. A government leaflet called *Thinking about childminding?* starts with the words 'Imagine a job that makes a real, positive difference to a child's life'. Whether you choose to be a childminder or a nanny, you will:

- help children to
  - find out about the world they live in
  - develop in a healthy way
  - learn new skills
- watch them grow in confidence, enjoying the company of other children and adults
- play a part in providing them with a sound foundation for their future lives.

The decision to work in a home-based setting adds something extra. You will:

- have close individual relationships with both children and families, getting to know them well over a period of time
- become a special person to the children, and to their parents too.

A special person

A registered childminder is someone who looks after one or more children under the age of eight (12 in Scotland and Northern Ireland) for more than two hours a day in the childminder's own home, for reward. They are self-employed, but they must be registered.

Nannies work in the homes of children and families. They may live in with the family, or come to work daily, and they may share their time between two or more families. They are employed by the family. They do not have to be registered but, in England, they can go through a voluntary government approval process.

Childminders who care only for children aged over seven cannot be registered, but in England they can choose to be approved.

This book covers similar ground to the Introduction to Childcare Practice (home-based) course (ICP) so you should find it a useful companion to the course. Links to specific parts of the course are shown throughout the book by the symbol shown on the right of this page.

Link to ICP
Section

The ICP course is the first of five units that make up the CACHE Level 3 Diploma in Home-based Childcare (DHC). This chart shows how each chapter links to sections of the ICP course.

Section of ICP course	Covered in chapter
1. Establishing a safe and healthy childcare environment in a home-based setting	
a) Assess and take appropriate action to ensure the home environment is safe for children of different ages and stages of development	4
b) Select appropriate equipment to meet the needs of children of different ages and ensure that it is safe for use	4
c) Maintain equipment according to manufacturer's guidance	4
d) Supervise children appropriately, according to their stage of development and the activities they are doing, both in and outside the home	4
e) Safeguard children outside the home by	4
• observing road safety and relevant legislation when travelling with children by car and other modes of transport	
• assessing the safety of playgrounds and other outdoor environments	
f) Maintain a clean and safe home environment by knowing how to	4
• use hygienic work practices	
• dispose of all waste materials safely	
• store and prepare food safely	
• assess risk in relation to pets	

Introduction

Section of ICP course	Covered in chapter

g) Plan how to respond to accidents and incidents by
  • making your own personal emergency plan
  • recording accidents and incidents
  • practising evacuation procedures with the children
	4

h) Understand the importance of having a current first aid qualification for babies and young children	3, 4
i) Know about the safe storage and administration of medicines	4
2. Establishing routines for home-based childcare	
a) The importance of establishing a routine for the child's day and of taking account of parent's wishes	5, 7

b) Planning and implementing routines which meet the needs of children of different ages and stages of development, including
  • arrivals and departures
  • taking children to and from school and playgroup/pre-school
  • meal and snack times
  • sleep and rest periods
  • children's play and activities
  • taking children out and about
  • homework and early evening activities for school-age children
	5

3. Providing play and other activities for children in a home-based setting	
a) The importance of play as a part of children and young people's learning and all round development	5
b) Promoting development through play	5
c) What you can learn about children from observing their behaviour and play	5
d) Planning play and activities in the home, including using household items and domestic activities	5
e) The availability and value of other resources, including libraries, drop-ins, toy libraries and equipment loan schemes	5
4. Introducing children and their families to your childcare service	
a) The importance of working in partnership with parents for the well-being of the child	7
b) The importance of sharing information with parents and ways to do this	7, 8

Section of ICP course	Covered in chapter
c) The effects on children of different ages and their families of the transition from the family home to other childcare setting or carer	7
d) The importance of preparing the child and their family for this change	7
e) Strategies to prepare and support the child and parents during the settling in period	7
f) The importance of effective communication with parents and children	7, 8, 9
5. Managing children's behaviour in the home-based setting	
a) Factors which influence children's behaviour, including behaviour related to particular stages of child development (i.e. toddler tantrums, difficulties during transition from carer to carer or from one environment to another)	8
b) The importance of consistency of care between the home-based practitioner and the parents	8
c) How to develop and share a framework for children's behaviour such as 'house rules' and 'setting agreed boundaries'	7
d) Strategies to promote positive behaviour and respond to challenging behaviour	8
6. Inclusion and anti-bias practice	
a) The importance of valuing each child as an individual	5
b) Understanding that children develop and learn as individuals	5
c) The effects of prejudice and stereotyping on children	5
d) The importance of the home-based practitioner being a positive role model to the children	5
e) Creating an environment in which all children feel welcomed, respected and included	5
7. Child protection in the home-based setting	
a) Definitions and types of abuse to include physical, emotional and sexual abuse and neglect	9
b) Common signs and symptoms of possible abuse.	9
c) Understanding the nature and extent of child abuse	9
d) Empowering children to protect themselves and to understand that they have rights	9
e) Bullying: recognition, prevention, supporting children and appropriate action	9
f) Your responsibilities if you suspect that a child may have been abused, including • the action that your local authority requires you to take if you suspect abuse	9

Section of ICP course	Covered in chapter
• any specific local guidance and procedures • the importance of making a written record of what you have observed g) The vulnerability of practitioners, and in the case of childminders, their families, to allegations of abusing children, the importance of keeping records of incidents, and where and how to seek advice	9
8. Starting a home-based childcare service	
a) Current, relevant legislation and the role of regulatory bodies	3
b) The importance of effective record-keeping and the information that needs to be kept on the child and their family	7, 9
c) How to negotiate and agree a contract with parents	7
d) Sharing information, confidentiality and data protection	8
e) Financial planning in setting rates for childcare services	6
f) How to maintain accurate financial records, including deductible costs, and, in the case of childminders, to meet statutory requirements	6
g) The importance of having written policies if required by law, sources of help and guidance	6
h) The importance of having adequate public liability insurance cover	6
i) How to market your childcare service effectively	6
j) Sources of support and information on setting up and running your childcare service	1, 3, 9
k) Information about continuing professional development, training and quality assurance	10

CHAPTER I

How it will affect my life

This chapter will help you assess the implications of starting work as a home-based childcarer.

Starting a new job always brings many changes, and deciding to work as a childminder or nanny will have an impact on the whole of your life. This chapter looks at:

- the likely implications of your choice of job
- making a commitment
- some early decisions you need to make.

Implications for childminders

For childminders, there are effects on your own family and home, and your personal time.

Spotlight on practice

Katrina's children are Molly (two), Alex (six) and Rob (nine), her partner is Jason, their cat is Mortimer, and her father, Doug, lives just round the corner. Katrina decided to become a childminder, and she started to give some thought to how it would affect her family and home life. Her decision was influenced by wanting to earn some money but also to be at home with Molly and for Alex and Rob out of school hours and terms, but she also realised that:

- she would need to be very organised first thing in the morning to make sure her family had their breakfast and were ready to go to work and school in time, so she could be ready to greet the children that she would be looking after

- she would have to plan how to fit shopping, cleaning, washing, ironing, gardening and preparing family meals around her childminding work

- she would be working long hours and would have to be careful about making sure she could fit in going to the hairdresser and dentist, and also working for her qualifications – and time for her family and herself

- Jason would need some peace and quiet to sleep in on the mornings following his occasional night shifts

- Molly would need some careful preparation for the arrival of the children Katrina was childminding – she would take time to adjust to sharing her mum and her toys (and Mortimer might need some attention too)

- Doug would have to understand that he must not smoke when the children Katrina was childminding were around

- Alex and Rob would need to store their precious possessions away in their bedroom.

▶

Storing precious items away

Katrina and Jason talked about how childminding would affect all the family, and Jason was very positive about her decision. He felt all the family would enjoy having extra children around, once they had adjusted to the changes. They mentioned the plans to their neighbours. Some were concerned about lots of cars coming and going, but Katrina explained that only small numbers of families would be involved. Others said that they were used to the children in the area playing outside and didn't think it would be a problem – but they were pleased to be consulted.

Implications for nannies

For nannies, there are issues about working (and possibly living) in someone else's home.

Spotlight on practice

Shona was looking for a job as a nanny. She had decided that she wanted to live in, so as to have the benefits of no accommodation or travel costs. She talked to some established nannies and decided that she must discuss the following points carefully with potential employers:

- that she saw her role as responsibility for all aspects of the children's care including taking them to and from school and pre-school, to the dentist and swimming classes, preparing their meals and washing and ironing their clothes, **but** she did not see cleaning the house, doing the whole family's laundry or getting meals for the parents as part of her job

- their expectations about the hours she would be available, and understanding that when she was off duty, her time was her own

- that she would want her room to be private and she wouldn't expect the parents or children to come in unless invited

- that she would want to be able to have her friends over to visit her when she was off duty – of course, respecting the family's privacy, routines and bedtimes.

This helped her to be confident about going for interviews and clarifying things in a pleasant way with parents from the start.

Commitment

Home-based childcare is not a job to enter into unless you are prepared to make a commitment. Parents need reliable childcare arrangements that will last, and will depend on you to help them maintain their working and family responsibilities. Children need continuity in their lives, and suffer from disruption if their childcare changes often or suddenly.

Think about it!

Are you able and prepared to commit yourself to providing a reliable service to families over a reasonable period of time? Can you foresee anything that might prevent you making a professional time commitment?

Decision time

You should make some decisions before you start looking for your first customers.

▷ Take action!

Decide: What age group of children do you want to work with?

Some home-based carers are willing to work across a wide age range, from new babies to teenagers, but others have a variety of reasons for choosing a particular age group.

I only want to work with pre-school children. I have my own children at home during the school holidays, and if there were any other older children, I'd feel overwhelmed.

Ruth

> I like the company of school-age children, and I'm building up my skills to work with older disabled children.
>
> **Jon**

> I don't feel I want to take on babies. I find the routines they need a bit restricting and I enjoy children more when they get to the chatty stage.
>
> **Malathy**

Make your choices to suit:

* your personal and family circumstances
* your strengths – the skills you feel you can offer a particular age group
* what you will find enjoyable – the children will have more fun too.

> I'm great with toddlers

> The children are all at school

> The routine will suit me

Make choices to suit you

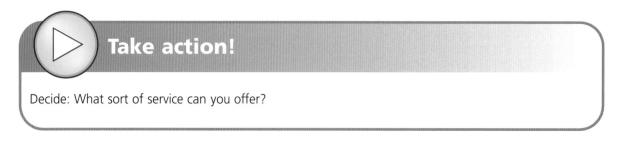

▷ Take action!

Decide: What sort of service can you offer?

There are many variations in the home-based childcare service you may be able and willing to offer, and you need to decide in advance how you want to work.

⚠ Think about it!

Think about whether you will offer your services full-time or part-time, and what your starting and finishing times will be, bearing in mind parents' working patterns. Will you offer overnight and/or weekend care (if you are a childminder, you will need to make sure your registration permits you to take on overnight care)? Will your service be available in school holidays?

If you're a nanny, do you want to work in a rural or urban area? Would you be prepared to work overseas? If you're a childminder, which schools and pre-schools can you offer to take children to and from? Can you take children to clubs and classes in your area (this may partly depend on whether you have a car or can drive)?

▷ Take action!

Decide: Do you want to work on your own or with someone else?

For many people, their choice of home-based childcare as a job is linked to their wish to be their own boss and be able to work independently. But some childminders work with another registered childminder, an assistant or a student helper, and sometimes a family employs more than one nanny.

There are advantages of working with other people. You have someone else to share planning and organising the work, you provide company for one another and you have someone else to help you sort out any problems or uncertainties. However, you do need to make sure you can get on with the other person and take a similar approach to working. Wife–husband and mother–daughter teams can be very successful, but work disagreements can also spill over into personal relationships. A childminder who takes on an assistant becomes an employer, with all the responsibilities that this involves.

? Learning more

NCMA's members' handbook *Running your Childminding Business* contains detailed advice on working with others, and their *Working as a Nanny* publication looks at all the options open to nannies. (These publications are only available to members of the National Childminding Association, NCMA.)

Looking for support

Link to ICP
Section 8j

Whatever plans and choices you make, you are likely to find some unexpected challenges. Many people find starting a new job quite stressful, and if you are working on your own, it can be difficult to find someone to share worries or problems with.

You may be able to get advice, information and reassurance from a local authority early years and childcare support or development worker. And the national organisations can provide you with a link to their local staff and members (see the Useful contacts section at the end of this book). Don't struggle on alone when there are experienced people ready to help you sort things out. The national organisations involved in childcare are the National Childminding Association which covers England and Wales (NCMA), Scottish Childminding Association (SCMA) and Northern Ireland Childminding Association (NICMA).

CHAPTER 2

What I can bring to the work

This chapter will help you get an overview of the qualities, knowledge and skills required to be a home-based childcarer.

Home-based childcare is rewarding work, but it is also challenging. This chapter looks at the knowledge and skills needed and gives you a chance to think about what you have to offer.

Home-based childcarers must be able to:

- plan the routine of the children's day
- provide activities and experiences for children to help them play and learn
- keep children safe and healthy
- manage children's behaviour
- work in partnership with parents
- work with children and families from a diverse range of cultural and social backgrounds
- protect children from abuse
- handle the business side of their role.

To do all of the above things successfully and in ways that benefit the children, you need certain personal qualities, as well as knowledge and skills. If you are a parent, you may already have a good foundation of necessary knowledge and skills, but you will need to extend it to the care of other people's children.

Think about it!

Take a look at the qualities, knowledge and skills listed below and think about how many you already have, and which you will need to develop further (tick the relevant column).

Qualities	I feel confident about this	I'll need to develop this more
Enjoy being with children		
Patient and caring		
Sense of humour		
Able to be flexible		
Calm		
Receptive to new ideas and willing to learn		
Respectful of cultures and backgrounds different from my own		

▶

Energetic and enthusiastic		
Stamina and good health		
Knowledge		
Know how to meet the needs of children, whatever their ethnic, cultural or family background or disability		
Know how to help children develop and learn		
Know how to support parents		
Know how to keep children safe and healthy and protect them from harm		
Skills		
Able to communicate with children		
Able to communicate with adults		
Business-like and professional		
Able to keep confidences		
Well organised		
Able to work with children of different ages		

Being able to communicate with children is an essential part of childcaring

Don't worry if you feel that you still have a way to go before being able to do all of this! Reading this book is your first step in building up your knowledge and skills as a professional home-based childcarer, and there will be many opportunities for you to learn more, through reading more, attending courses and meeting other people in your profession. What matters is being honest about what you don't yet know and being aware of any aspects of your practice as a home-based childcarer that you can build on and keep improving.

CHAPTER 3

The formalities of registration/approval

This chapter will help you to ensure that you comply with the laws and regulations associated with home-based childcare.

Before you can begin work as a home-based childcarer, you must make sure that you comply with the laws and regulations which set the standards for home-based childcare. This chapter looks at:

- the formal procedures you will have to go through to become either a registered childminder or an approved home-based childcarer
- joining a professional organisation.

Registration as a childminder

Link to ICP
Sections 8a, 1h

If you intend to become a childminder caring for children aged under eight, the law requires you to be registered. Your first step is to make contact with the regulatory body for your country:

- in England, this is the Office for Standards in Education (Ofsted)
- in Wales, this is the Care Standards Inspectorate for Wales (CSIW)
- in Scotland, this is the Scottish Commission for the Regulation of Care
- in Northern Ireland, this is your local Health and Social Services Trust.

See the Useful contacts section at the end of this book for details. The regulatory bodies publish the national standards you have to meet in order to be registered, and the procedures you have to go through.

Arrangements vary a little between the four countries, but you are likely to find that you will be invited to a pre-registration briefing session where you will have the chance to find out the details of what is involved in becoming a childminder and the standards you will have to meet. You will have to:

- complete an application form
- apply to the Criminal Records Bureau (CRB) for an 'enhanced disclosure' for yourself and every adult member (over 16) of your household (you will receive information about how to do this)
- arrange a health check with your GP (and perhaps a social services check, and/or a reference)
- receive a visit from an inspector to discuss with you how you will meet the registration standards
- pay a registration fee.

When you have done all of this and satisfied the regulatory body that you can meet the necessary standards and are a suitable person to be a childminder, you will be issued with a certificate which confirms that you are a registered childminder. It should not take you more than three to six months to get registered. If you find it is taking longer, contact NCMA, SCMA or NICMA.

In the future, you will be inspected by the regulatory body, and you should make sure you have the necessary information about when and how this will happen.

In England and Wales, you have to complete an introductory course about childminding and also a first aid course within six months of starting childminding. Courses are run in most areas, and most new childminders complete Introduction to Childcare Practice – home-based (ICP), which is the first unit of the Council for Awards in Children's Care and Education (CACHE) qualification, the Diploma in Home-based Childcare. To find out more about this qualification, contact CACHE – you will find their details in the Useful contacts section at the end of this book. This book covers similar ground to ICP so you should find it a useful companion to the course.

Keep a first aid box in your home

Your first aid course must be one specifically for people who work with young children. Suitable courses are run by the Red Cross, St. John Ambulance and other first aid trainers. Your local Children's Information Service or NCMA will be able to give you details of when ICP and first aid courses are available in your area (see Useful contacts).

In the first aid course you will learn about:
• how to respond to an emergency
• techniques of resuscitation
• how to deal with
   ◦ burns and scalds
   ◦ fractures and head injuries
   ◦ poisoning
   ◦ bleeding
   ◦ anaphylactic shock
• what you need in your first aid box
• keeping records of accidents
• dealing with children who become ill, and giving medication to children.

▶ Take action!

When you have a copy of the standards you will have to comply with as a registered childminder, spend time going through them carefully to find out what they tell you about:

- how many children of varying ages you will be allowed to care for at any one time
- safety and hygiene of your childminding setting, including smoking
- providing children with play and learning opportunities
- outdoor play space
- managing children's behaviour
- working in partnership with parents
- keeping records
- promoting equality of opportunity and anti-discriminatory practice
- child protection
- providing food and drink
- children who are ill and giving children medication.

To be ready for registration, you will need to be very familiar with the standards, and give careful thought to how you will measure up to them, but you may be feeling a bit overwhelmed by all you need to do to achieve this, and want some information, advice and support, and some practical help with the forms and regulations. In England and in parts of Scotland, a scheme called 'Support Childminding' has been set up to help by putting you in touch with an experienced childminder in your area.

Support from an experienced childminder

Your local authority, or NCMA or SCMA, will be able to tell you about how the scheme works in your area. In Wales, mentoring sessions are laid on by NCMA to help with completing the forms and preparing the necessary documents.

You can also get help from your local childminding group, and from the national organisations, NCMA, SCMA and NICMA.

> *I can't think how I would have got through my registration without the help of my support childminder. She was so friendly, full of information and kept reassuring me that it would be fine.*
>
> **Nadia**

Approved home-based childcarers

Link to ICP
Section 8j

In England, if you want to work as a nanny or as a childminder caring only for children aged over seven, you cannot be registered by Ofsted (Office for Standards in Education), but you can become an approved childcarer. Parents may be keen for you to go through the approval process so that they can claim the childcare element of the Working Tax Credit, or get help with childcare costs from their employer.

To be approved, you must:

- either already hold a relevant qualification or attend an induction course (such as ICP – see the previous section for childminders)
- hold a current first aid certificate for babies and young children (see the previous section)
- have an 'enhanced disclosure' from the Criminal Records Bureau (CRB)
- be at least 18 years old
- pay a fee.

Approved childcarers have to be re-approved every year.

Learning more

For more information and to get application forms telephone 0845 767 8111 or visit www.childcareapprovalscheme.co.uk.

Joining a professional organisation

Link to ICP
Section 8j

As you set out on your new profession as a home-based childcarer, you should give careful thought to joining a professional organisation.

The National Childminding Association (NCMA) offers membership in England and Wales to registered childminders, nannies and other approved childcarers. They provide the usual benefits of membership of a professional body. The Scottish and Northern Ireland Childminding Associations offer a similar range of benefits to their members.

But perhaps the most important reason for joining is to be part of your profession and be able to contribute to its future development. You can achieve this by contributing to the powerful and effective voice of NCMA and its sister organisations which have nearly 30 years of experience in representing the interests of home-based childcarers to government and the media.

Benefits of NCMA membership include:

- a handbook and a regular magazine
- discounts on a wide range of publications
- an information phone line
- public liability insurance (a legal requirement for registered childminders and very important for nannies) and tailor-made, good value home and car insurance
- free legal advice and representation
- special deals on health insurance, loans and car rescue.

▶ Take action!

Send off for information about NCMA, SCMA or NICMA, and consider the benefits of membership as you embark on your new job.

CHAPTER 4

Safe and sound

This chapter will help you check that the environment you offer children is safe and healthy and that you work in ways to keep them safe from harm.

4 Safe and sound

One of your basic responsibilities as a home-based childcarer is to make sure that the environment you offer children is safe and hygienic, and another is to think about how to work in ways which keep the children you care for safe from harm. This chapter looks at:

- risks
- the balanced approach
- hygiene
- equipment and practice
- supervision
- going out and about
- emergencies.

Risks

Link to ICP
Section 1a

Every year in the UK, around two million children are taken to hospital accident and emergency departments as a result of accidents. Almost every day a child dies in an accident. Young children have not yet learned what is dangerous to them and need you to protect them from possible accidents. As children grow and mature, your role is to help them understand how to manage risks and keep themselves safe.

Hygiene is important because children's immune systems take a while to develop in their early years, so they are vulnerable to infections.

Whether you are a childminder working in your own home, or a nanny working in a family's home, you need to carry out a risk assessment before you start caring for children in that environment. This means taking a long hard look at the home, room by room, plus the garden, and spotting potential hazards. And when you have seen where all the potential dangers are, you need to decide what changes to make. If you are a childminder, you will be able to go ahead and make the changes, but if you are a nanny, you will have to discuss your concerns with the parents and plan together what to do. (You may find it helpful to show them the Sure Start publication (2005) *Employing an approved childcarer*.)

Spotlight on practice

Chrissie was planning to become a childminder so she carried out a risk assessment on her home. Her own children were all aged over seven, but she was expecting to care for toddlers aged 18 months and upwards, so she thought back to how vulnerable such young children are to accidents. She realised that she would need to:

- get two stair-gates – one for the top of the stairs and one to put across the kitchen door
- fix some 'gripper' backing on the slippery rugs on her polished hall floor
- put child-resistant socket covers on the power points
- have her rickety garden fence repaired and get a new fastening on the garden gate.

Gemma had agreed to become a nanny for a family with a 4-month-old baby and a 2-year-old toddler. Before she joined the family, she spent some time looking carefully at the family's house and she found that:

- an open fire was sometimes lit in the sitting room in the winter, but there was no fireguard

- the family's pets' feeding dishes and litter trays were within easy reach of the toddler
- the pond in the back garden did not have a cover
- there were a lot of gardening, car maintenance and DIY equipment and materials in the garden shed but the fastening was broken.

You might spot other hazards when you carry out your risk assessment, such as:

- large areas of glass or low level glass which are not made of safety glass (toughened or laminated) or covered by safety film
- spaces between banisters on the staircase that leave room for a child to fall or squeeze through, or get their head trapped
- loose wires trailing from rotary clothes lines or cords from curtains or blinds.

▷ Take action!

Carry out a risk assessment in the environment where you will be working with children, and make a list of the changes you plan to make or to discuss with parents. (It may help you to spot the danger points in a room if you get down to toddler height – you will be able to see the electric flexes trailing temptingly over the edge of the kitchen unit, or the table cloth just waiting to be pulled off, flower vase and all!)

Carry out a risk assessment in your home

One action you are very likely to have to take is to check that any objects and materials which could be harmful to children are stored out of sight and reach of the children. You may also need to put house plants, such as ones with trailing stems and poisonous ones, on high shelves, out of children's reach.

Harmful objects and materials to store away might be:

- medicines and tablets
- matches and sharp objects such as knives and razor blades
- household cleaners
- polythene bags
- alcohol and cigarettes.

Making a risk assessment and improving the safety of your working environment is not something that you do just once. Childminders will take on new children; the children you care for will grow and develop so the risks for them will change, so you need to repeat the exercise every few months. And you will need to check at the beginning of each day that your safety arrangements are being maintained – it's all too easy for another member of the household to leave a stair-gate at the top of a flight of stairs unfastened.

Learning more

The NCMA guide to children's safety (2005) is a valuable resource for all home-based childcarers, and NCMA also provides nanny members with a special risk assessment checklist.

The balanced approach

Parents trust you to keep their children safe, but if you are over-protective, children will not learn an important skill for adult life – how to protect themselves from harm. You have to protect them, but also give them the chance to have experiences which might be risky if they don't learn to manage and reduce the risks. You may feel that you must be very protective of young children and of disabled children, but this could be doing them no favours.

Children need to try out new activities and have experiences which are challenging so they can learn about the world around them, and explore and discover for themselves. If the adults who look after them are over-anxious, continually fuss over them and won't let them try out new things, they can become over-cautious and miss out on valuable and fun activities. Some learning experiences involve risk, but you allow children to try out new and challenging experiences so they can develop and

Some learning experiences involve risk

progress. It's quite risky for babies to roll over or to pull themselves up on furniture, but you won't prevent them taking those risks because you know they need to develop and progress.

If you remove all risk from children's lives and 'wrap them up in cotton wool', you will also get in the way of their learning about potential dangers and how to handle them. Adults take risks all the time (crossing the road, walking downstairs) but we have learned how to reduce risks and avoid accidents; children need to learn this too. Tune in to how far they are able to take care of themselves and how much they still rely on an adult to foresee danger. This depends not only on their age, but also on their personality — some children (and adults) are more reckless than others. And children with learning difficulties sometimes do not understand danger and need adults to go on protecting them for longer.

You have to achieve a balance between preventing accidents and making sure children do things which enable them to become confident and able to look after themselves.

If you care for older children, you will have to let them try out challenging new experiences, but at the same time help them to understand potential dangers and how to avoid them.

Hygiene – keep it clean

Link to ICP
Section 1f

If you are a childminder, of course you keep your home clean for your own family. If you are a nanny, you will be joining a family who keep their home clean. But you should consider adopting a more rigorous approach to hygiene, to meet professional standards. You don't have to create a clinically sterile environment (there is some evidence that children who are in environments that are 'too clean' develop more allergies), but you must be careful to take sensible precautions at all times to make sure that children don't contract infections.

Think about it!

Think about:

- keeping work surfaces, implements and utensils used for preparing food, and tea towels really clean
- running the fridge at 4°C–5°C, and the freezer at minus 18°C (to stop bacteria multiplying)
- emptying rubbish bins frequently and cleaning them thoroughly
- disinfecting the seat and handle of the toilet, the door handle and taps in the toilet/bathroom regularly
- always wrapping disposable nappies individually and putting them in the dustbin outside the house as soon as possible, not in the kitchen bin
- never allowing pets onto working surfaces
- washing up and storing pets' feeding bowls separately from utensils used by humans.

You will need to be scrupulous in your hygiene when preparing and cooking food, for example:

- cover or wrap food in the fridge and keep raw meat at the bottom (to prevent blood and bacteria dripping onto other foods)
- never use food after the use-by dates
- take care to defrost frozen food fully before cooking
- never refreeze food that has been thawed.

❓ Learning more

Find out about any food hygiene courses that run in your area – contact the local college or NCMA, SCMA or NICMA.

Make sure your practice protects children by:

- never putting a baby's dummy back into its mouth after it has fallen onto the floor without washing and sterilising it first
- having a separate flannel and towel for each child, and laundering them regularly
- never changing babies or putting toddlers on the potty in the kitchen, always tipping the potty down the toilet (not the hand basin), and always rinsing and disinfecting the potty after use.

Children can learn hygiene habits from a very early age, and they will learn best from your example of washing your hands before eating and after:

- handling raw food
- going to the toilet
- changing nappies
- coughing or sneezing, or wiping children's noses
- touching pets or their feeding bowls, bedding, litter trays, etc.

Talk to them about how germs can make us poorly if we don't wash our hands.

If there are pets in the home, make sure that:

- the floor is cleaned up carefully after a pet has been fed (to prevent bacteria multiplying or pests being attracted)
- any pet food stored in the fridge is well covered
- animals are kept clear of fleas, wormed and inoculated
- dogs are exercised away from the garden
- the sand pit is covered when it's not in use to prevent animals from getting into it.

Setting a good example

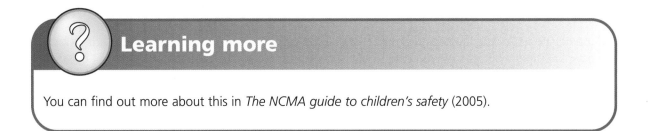

? Learning more

You can find out more about this in *The NCMA guide to children's safety* (2005).

Equipment and practice

Some of the actions you will need to take as a result of your risk assessment will be to get and use safety equipment such as childproof locks for cupboard doors, smoke alarms and a fire blanket or extinguisher. It is not a good idea to buy safety equipment like car seats from second hand shops, or car boot or nearly new sales where you can't be sure of the quality and safety of the equipment for sale.

Link to ICP
Sections 1b, 1c

But just getting the equipment is not enough. You must make sure you use it consistently and properly: it is your daily practice which matters most. There is no point in having straps on the buggy or high chair if you regularly forget to fix them.

You will also use equipment:

- for play and learning, indoors and out (construction toys, climbing frames, computers, painting easels)
- for childcare (high chair, bottle sterilising equipment)
- to transport children (buggy, wheelchair, car seat or restraints).

When you buy new equipment, always check for safety standards markings, such as the British Standards Institute (BSI), or the European Union CE mark or the British standard number (BS EN XXXX).

Kitemark® of the British Standards Institution (BSI)

Lion mark

CE mark

Look out for these safety marks on toys and equipment

All this equipment can be used in a safe or unsafe way and, again, it is your practice that is important. Remember to:

- use equipment as the manufacturer says it should be used. For example, it is very important to know how to unfold a buggy so that all the safety clips are in place – otherwise the buggy might collapse and trap a child inside, possibly injuring them
- use equipment which is suitable and safe for the size and stage of development of a particular child, not too small or too big – either can be dangerous. For example, it would be unsafe to put an 18-month-old baby into a car seat designed for a 4-year-old child. Look out for age warning symbols on toys which say things like 'not suitable for children under 36 months'

- make regular checks of toys for sharp edges, pieces working loose, etc. and repair them or throw them away; check that swings don't work loose; check that brakes are working on prams and buggies.

? Learning more

You can find out more about this in *The NCMA guide to children's safety,* or by visiting the following BSI weblink: www.bsieducation.org/Education/downloads/publications/ChildcareleafletsIssue3.pdf

There are some forms of equipment which you should think carefully about using at all. The Child Accident Prevention Trust (CAPT) advises that you should not use babywalkers because they lead to so many accidents. They can tip over steps or get caught under a radiator or against a door – and tip the baby out. And there is evidence that they actually hamper children's progress as walkers because they don't put their full weight on their legs and feet.

Some aspects of your safety practice matter for the safety of all children, but matter even more for disabled children. For example, many accidents happen because children (and adults) trip over toys left on the floor of play areas, but it is especially important for a child with a visual impairment that floor surfaces are kept clear and that furniture and equipment is always kept in the same position.

Keep floor areas clear

Supervision

An important part of your practice in maintaining children's safety and well-being is to supervise them.

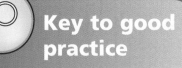

Link to ICP
Section 1d

They may need:

- constant supervision: this means you watch them every moment, perhaps in direct contact with them
- close supervision: this means you watch them most of the time, ready to step in and take action if their safety is put at risk
- general supervision: this means you check on them regularly, and keep a 'watchful eye' from a distance.

Supervise according to what children are doing

Key to good practice

How much supervision you give children at any time depends on:

✓ their stage of development and understanding (an inquisitive toddler needs more supervision than a calm 7-year-old)

✓ what they are doing (a child learning to use a sharp knife is likely to need constant supervision)

✓ where they are (a visually impaired child may need closer supervision when they are outside the familiar home setting)

✓ changes in the surroundings (when it's been raining or it's icy, outdoor play equipment may be slippery so you need to supervise children more closely).

Out and about

**Link to ICP**
Section 1e

You will be taking the children out of the home setting to widen their horizons and expand their learning opportunities. Outings may be just a regular visit to the local library or shops, or special outings to the seaside or city farm. You need to think about how to transport them safely by car, and safety issues when you're out walking.

If you're taking children in a car, you need to make sure you have the right type and size of seat or restraint for each child, according to their size. And once again, it isn't just the right equipment which will protect the children, but your practice – you must always fasten the children in securely, even for the shortest journeys. Always get children in and out of the car on the pavement side, and put the little ones into the pram or buggy before the bigger ones get out (put the big ones in the car first for the return journey). Make sure that your car insurance covers you for transporting the children you work with.

Match the equipment to the height and weight of the children

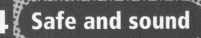

Walking alongside a road is a potentially very dangerous situation for children, and you will have to be very firm about them holding on to the buggy and staying close to you, on the inside of the pavement. Reins give toddlers freedom to walk along without the discomfort of keeping their arm up in the air to hold an adult's hand. Bear in mind that children become more vulnerable to road accidents from about the age of seven, when adults tend to keep a less careful eye on them. Always cross roads in a safe place, preferably at a pedestrian crossing, and talk to the children about watching carefully for traffic and waiting for the green man to appear.

Think about it!

Imagine you are caring for a 14-month-old baby and a 3-year-old, and are going to collect a 6-year-old and an 8-year-old from school. Think how you would manage the journeys in either direction safely, whether you were doing this by car, or on foot.

You will sometimes take children to play in a local park or playground. Choose one where:

- there are special areas for the younger children, free from broken glass, syringes and dogs' mess
- there are bark chippings or matting under the play equipment
- the equipment is well maintained.

Further afield

If you're going to be out and about for a whole day, there are a range of things to plan ahead to ensure children's safety and well-being.

Key to good practice

If you're planning to take children on an outing:

✓ choose an outing which will be suitable for the age/stage of development of the children and that they will find interesting and enjoyable. When children are bored they may begin to behave in foolish and unsafe ways

✓ make sure you give parents the full details about the outing beforehand and get written permission from every child's parents

✓ if you are travelling by public transport, double check timetables (especially for the return journey!)

✓ draw up a checklist of everything you need to take with you.

Spotlight on practice

When Phil was planning to take the children to the seaside for the day, his checklist looked like this:

- food and drink
- first aid supplies, sun cream
- mobile phone and parents' contact phone numbers (in case we're delayed on the way back)
- nappies and changing equipment; wet wipes, tissues; spare clothing, including sun hats and waterproofs
- the buggy and the reins
- a blanket to sit on
- money for fares and entrance fee to the aquarium
- maps, timetables - we don't want to get lost or stranded!

Emergencies

Link to ICP
Sections 1g, 1h, 1i

Despite all your best efforts, accidents may occur when you are looking after children. Your first aid course should have prepared you for how to deal with an emergency, and you must develop your personal emergency plan. This should include making sure that:

- you have easy access to a telephone
- you have made arrangements with someone who can care for the children if you have to leave them (if you have to take one to hospital, or if you are the emergency)
- you put important phone numbers (children's parents' home and work, and your emergency back-up person) somewhere where you can find them immediately
- your first aid box is properly equipped, as you learned on your first aid course
- you explain your emergency plan to parents, so they know what you plan to do if there is an emergency and what you will expect them to do, and avoid confusion if you ever need to put the plans into action.

> *Looking back, it was dreadful when Charlie fell off the slide and broke his arm. But somehow I kept my cool. I had the list of parents' contact numbers by the phone so I was able to get hold of his dad right away and arrange to meet him at the hospital. I phoned my mum, as we had arranged, and she came round immediately to look after the other children.*
>
> **Asmita**

Key to good practice

Remember:

✓ the importance of recording all accidents, however minor – you never know how serious an injury may turn out to be

✓ only give children medication with the written permission of their parents

✓ get the parents to sign and date all reports of accidents and records of medication you give, to show that you informed them.

Besides accidents, you need to think about what you would do if there was a fire or other emergency.

Think about it!

How would you evacuate children from your home-based setting if a fire broke out – in the hall, or upstairs? Think about:

- babies asleep upstairs or crawling about downstairs
- just-walking toddlers
- pre-school children
- older children.

Make a plan of how to practise your evacuation plan with children regularly, without frightening them and making them think that something terrible is about to happen.

Learning more

You can learn more about children's health in Unit 2 of the Diploma in Home-based Childcare (DHC).

CHAPTER 5

Planning to work with children

This chapter will help you plan ahead to provide routines for the children that meet the needs of different ages and stages of development.

As you prepare for your first few days and weeks of home-based childcare, you should begin to plan:

- the routines you will provide for the children
- the play activities and experiences you will provide for them
- how you will make sure you include all children in your home-based setting and give them equal chances to develop and learn.

This chapter will look at how and what you should plan.

Routines

Consistency is important to children, so you should aim to establish regular routines. But don't make your routines so rigid that there is no time for spontaneous fun!

Link to ICP
Sections 2a, 2b

Each home-based childcarer needs to provide a different routine, depending on the number of children you look after and their ages, and how long you look after them each day. Think how you will fit things into your day.

This may all sound busy and full of activity, but when you plan how to fit all these aspects of routines together, try to aim to create a relaxed feeling and unhurried pace in your home-based setting.

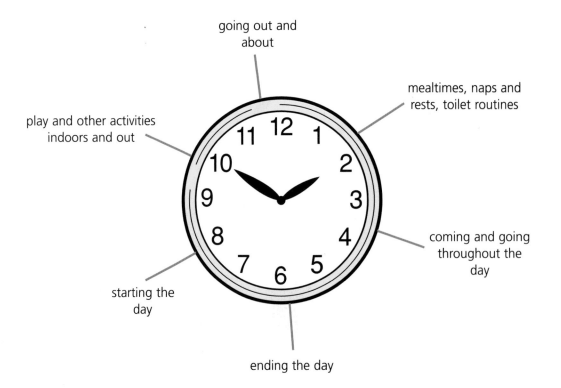

Starting the day

Whether you are looking after children in your home or theirs, you have to make an early start, and be alert and full of energy at the beginning of the day.

If you are a childminder, explain to members of your family that when parents and children arrive, you need to give them your undivided attention for a few minutes, because parents may have important information to give you about the child.

Key to good practice

If you are a childminder who wants to be seen as providing a professional service, you mustn't greet parents in your dressing gown! Just because you work in your own home, this doesn't mean you can present an appearance which looks as though you don't value yourself and your work.

Coming and going throughout the day

Your day will probably include taking children to and from pre-school/playgroup and school. Some school-age children may go to after-school activities such as music or dancing lessons, swimming or other sports, and if you have children of your own, you will also have to fit their activities into your schedule.

I am always amazed at how long it can take us to get out of the house. By the time we've put on our coats and hats, I've checked that everyone has 'been' and that they've all got their bags and stuff, and I've strapped the little ones into the buggy, I feel like I've done my day's work already!

Angie

Remember how long each task takes

Mealtimes, naps and rests, toilet routines

Sharing a meal is enjoyable and an important part of children's social development. Think about the timing of meals so that:

- children who start their days early in the morning don't get too hungry
- you can fit mealtimes in with pre-school, naps and other parts of your routine
- you don't rush the children through eating, but give them a relaxed atmosphere.

Key to good practice

Plan your timing carefully to make sure that children are not late (or too early) for school or left waiting at the end of the day.

Sharing a meal is part of social development

It's important to talk to parents about when children should have their rest or sleep. Some parents will want you to make sure that their child has a good long sleep during the day so they're awake in the early evening and the parents can enjoy their company. Other parents will be anxious that you don't let their child have a long sleep during the day. They want the child to get off to sleep in the evening so they can have time to themselves. Try to comply with parents' wishes as far as you can – though it's impossible to keep a sleepy child awake!

Key to good practice

Even something as simple as letting children have a nap or rest needs forethought.

✓ Make sure babies and toddlers have a quiet time and place to go to sleep.

✓ Find out what helps the child to fall asleep. Some children have a toy or 'cuddly' that is essential to them. Some want a light on when it gets dark, some want the curtains drawn. Some children drift off to a tape or like to be sung to – or massaged gently.

✓ Give older children quiet activities to do while the little ones sleep – it will help them recharge their batteries too.

✓ Be ready to adjust your routine as a baby grows into a toddler and needs a different pattern of sleep.

✓ Make sure you leave time in your schedule to wake children up quietly and without rush.

All children and toddlers differ in their patterns of sleep

Remember that older children often need a quiet time to rest and relax when they get in from school.

Make sure there is enough time in your daily routine so children are not hurried through toilet routines.

> *It's surprising how much time gets taken up with personal care routines – nappy changing or waiting for a toddler to use the potty, washing hands after the toilet and before meals, and so on. But these times are also times for chat and learning, and getting to know each little person.*
>
> Jo

Play and other activities, indoors and out

As you will see in the next part of this chapter, it is important for children to play, both indoors and out, and your routine must make sure they have extended periods of time for play. If you don't have access to a garden, plan regular trips to a park or playground.

Childminders don't do their main housework while they have the children in their care, and nannies don't normally do housework. But there are some household tasks which it is fine to do while the children are around as long as you always give children's needs and routines top priority. In fact, as you will see later in this chapter, involving children in simple domestic tasks can help them to learn.

Watching television can be used positively as a source of learning – it can widen children's perspectives on the world beyond their own experiences. And there's nothing wrong with using one of the children's favourite programmes or a video as an opportunity for you to relax and have a break in your tiring day.

Key to good practice

Ration the amount of viewing so it's one of many activities in the day, and don't have the TV on all the time ('moving wallpaper'). Try to watch programmes with the children so you can talk about what they've seen – and when the programme ends, say it's time to switch off and move on to something else.

Watch programmes with the children

Help and encouragement for homework

If a child has homework to do, discuss with parents whether they want the child to do it under your supervision or theirs. Make sure that you can provide a quiet time and place, and that you are able to give your attention to helping and encouraging them. Think about how the other children can be occupied at this time.

Going out and about

Home-based childcare has the advantage that you can take the children out often – it's much more difficult to arrange in a nursery. There are lots of opportunities for learning when you and the children venture out into your surrounding environment and community. For example:

- *Going for a walk* – some of your walks will be the essential ones to and from school, but going for a walk to the park or the library when you don't have to hurry gives you time to look at things and talk about what you see, like the window cleaner up his ladder, the leaves changing colour and the berries in autumn

- *Shopping* – don't try to do a big shop in a busy supermarket with children – they're likely to get tired and bored. But there are many learning opportunities in going into quieter shops to buy a few items, especially if you talk about what you're going to buy before you go and make a list. Children love to carry their own bags and hand over the money. Back home, unpacking what you've bought is a rich source of talk and learning, such as:

○ what colour is the packet that the biscuits are in?

○ which is heavier, the packet of breakfast cereal or the tin of tomatoes?

○ do you think we should put the butter in the cupboard or in the fridge?

• *Groups* – from an early age, children benefit from spending time with other children and playing in a group, but you may not have the room or equipment in your home-based setting to invite in several children (and sharing toys can become quite an issue!). Include sessions at group activities in your schedule so the children can have the chance to mix with other children, and you get the chance to meet other adults.

Take action!

Find out about what's available in your area – childminders' drop-ins, toddler groups, music, swimming or gym classes specially arranged for young children.

You may also take children on special outings occasionally, especially if you care for school-age children in the school holidays. Make sure when you choose somewhere for your outing that is going to be enjoyable and safe, especially if you have several young children, perhaps of different ages.

Ending the day

If you are a childminder, you may find that some children 'play up' when their parents arrive. You will need to agree with parents how you can work together to show the children you have shared expectations about their behaviour and which of you will deal with any unwanted behaviour.

If you are a nanny, you may be involved in bathtime and bedtime. It's important to go about this in a calm and soothing way, following a consistent routine. Stories and music can help children move gradually from the activities of the day to being ready to drift off to sleep.

Key to good practice

If you're going on an outing, you also need to think about:

✓ how you're going to travel – by car or public transport – and how long your journey is going to take

✓ getting parents' written permission

✓ preparing what you need to take with you – food, clothing, a first aid pack, mobile phone and information about contacting parents.

Bathtime can be a time to relax, ready for sleep

Key to good practice

Give the children some indication that their parents will soon be arriving or it's nearly time for bed. You could use rituals like clearing up to help to mark the time for children who are too young to understand 'clock time'.

Children's development and learning

There are many ways of looking at how children learn and develop, and one useful approach is the 'Seven Cs':

- Confidence
- Communication
- Co-ordination
- Concentration
- Competence
- Co-operation
- Creativity.

Formal learning depends on having a good foundation of development through:

- play
- everyday activities
- first-hand experiences
- talk

and each of these can be linked to the seven Cs.

? Learning more

You can learn more about children's development and how they learn by taking Unit 2 of the CACHE Diploma in Home-based Childcare.

Play, learning and development

Link to ICP
Sections 3a, 3b

Providing a variety of play activities and opportunities is an essential part of your role. Play is vitally important to children of all ages. Children are naturally curious and want to explore and experiment; play offers them the chance to do this. It helps them to:

- try out new skills and become more Confident in their abilities
- develop their imagination and Creativity
- learn to relate to other people – children and adults – and develop ways of Communicating
- understand their environment.

Play has a key role in early learning, but it goes on being important for children into their school years, complementing their formal learning at school. You may feel that it's not your role to 'teach' children, but you can't avoid being part of their learning, and offering them absorbing play activities is the best way you can help them develop.

Providing play activities and opportunities

Link to ICP
Sections 3b, 3d, 3e

⚠ Think about it!

How can you provide play activities in your home-based setting? Think about:

- storing toys and equipment so they are accessible to the children and they can choose for themselves, and help with putting away
- clear floor space
- table top space (with a wipe clean surface or plastic cover)
- access to play out of doors too, either in the garden or a park or playground.

You may have space for a specific play room or area, or you may provide play activities in the family living space. Don't feel you have to provide a mini-pre-school or nursery – it's important to maintain the home atmosphere.

Tidying up is part of learning and can be fun!

▶ Take action!

Check through this range of play activities and opportunities for children, and gather the resources (equipment and materials) you will need to be able to provide as many of them as possible, choosing those most suitable for the age of the children you look after and the space you have available.

Make-believe or imaginative play

Children love to play with:

- dressing up clothes and 'props' like a tea set, pots and pans, an iron and ironing board
- 'small world' toys like a garage, farm or doll's house
- dolls and puppets, Duplo or Playmobil people.

These all contribute to Creativity and, when children play together, Co-operation. They also enable children to play out roles and work through their emotions in ways which build their Confidence.

Make-believe play

Cutting and gluing encourages Co-operation, Creativity, Concentration and Co-ordination

Puzzles

Provide a variety of puzzles, from simple tray puzzles for toddlers to complicated jigsaws for school-age children to encourage Co-ordination and Concentration.

Construction sets

Wooden blocks, Lego and Stickle Bricks promote Co-ordination, Creativity and Concentration.

Drawing and painting

You will need large sheets of paper with:

- crayons, pencils and felt-tip pens
- paints and brushes.

Children of all ages enjoy drawing and painting and it develops Creativity and Co-ordination.

Junk modelling

Provide scissors and glue to make things from cardboard boxes, tubes and other recycled materials like fabric and pictures cut from catalogues – and add a bit of glitter for special occasions! (Let the children design their own; don't ask them to copy 'one you made earlier'.) Older children enjoy 'sticking' well into their school-age years and it encourages Creativity, Concentration and Co-ordination.

Books and videos

Make sure you have a variety of books and videos to cater for different stages of development, from card books for babies to reference books for school-age children. Books help to develop their Communication, Concentration and Creativity. Videos, like all television, should be used sparingly.

Shape sorters and threading toys

This sort of careful manipulation develops Co-ordination and Concentration.

Modelling

Plasticine can be enjoyable, but playdough is better (there are lots of different recipes: salt helps it to keep, and oil makes it soft) and helps children's Creativity, Concentration and Co-ordination.

Board games

You will need a variety of games, from simple picture lotto for pre-schoolers to more complicated games for school-age children to promote Co-operation and Communication.

Board games encourage Co-operation and Communication

Water or sand play

You may want to keep this outside – or maybe let some children join in with washing up (non-breakable and non-sharp things). Just providing containers for filling and pouring can encourage Co-ordination and Concentration.

Physical play

You may not have the funds to provide a climbing frame, slide and swing in the garden, or room for vigorous ball games. Where can you take the children to make sure they get the opportunity for this sort of play? They need it to build their Confidence and Co-ordination.

For babies

Babies enjoy exploring the contents of a treasure basket from the time they can sit, propped up on cushions. Collect a range of everyday objects made of natural materials (not plastic), put them in a good size basket and just let the baby take things out, look at them and find out what they're like. Include things like a wooden block, a length of metal chain, pieces of cloth with interesting textures (velvet, fur), a shell, brushes (nail brush, toothbrush), corks, a wooden clothes peg, a small mirror, metal lids of small containers, a wooden spoon, a bell. Make sure all the objects are clean because a baby's main way of finding out is via the mouth! You may be amazed how soon babies develop Concentration and Co-ordination.

Babies enjoy treasure baskets

5 Planning to work with children

You need to offer a variety of activities so you can maintain the children's interest and meet their needs at various stages of development. You also need to have tough, good-quality equipment – it will get a lot of use. But this doesn't mean you have to spend huge amounts of money on toys and play equipment – with a bit of imagination you can improvise playthings from household objects: cardboard boxes and saucepans with wooden spoons are very popular.

And, remember, the best play equipment a child of any age can have is an adult who gives them attention.

Everyday activities

There are also many opportunities for children's development and learning in everyday activities in the home setting. Children enjoy being involved in 'grown-up' tasks, and getting into the habit of clearing up after themselves is very valuable in building their Competence.

Learning from everyday activities

Everyday activities that help children's development and learning include:

- getting dressed and learning self-care skills such as feeding; going to the toilet and washing hands is the basis of Competence

- laying the table involves counting and sorting, and so does hanging out and bringing in washing

- helping to prepare food can develop eye/hand co-ordination and weighing ingredients for cooking is early maths

- watering plants and watching them grow is early science

- helping with the washing up is a form of water play (which can be calming and soothing).

First-hand experiences

Children can learn a lot from pictures in a book or on television, but these are second-hand experiences. It is difficult to make sense of pictures unless you have had real-world experiences to link them to. From their first hours of life, children start exploring the world around them, finding out about how things feel, taste, smell, look and sound. They go on learning from 'first-hand experiences' which give them direct access to objects and living creatures and stimulate their senses, such as:

- touching and feeling objects of differing textures – fabrics, furry animals, smooth and rough surfaces, sand (and mud!)
- tasting a variety of foods and smelling a variety of substances
- listening to many different sorts of sounds including all kinds of music
- looking carefully at all aspects of the environment – from tiny insects to large buildings
- experiencing all kinds of weather, throughout the seasons.

Throughout your working day, you can find ways of offering children first-hand experiences, especially when you go outdoors.

Talk

Children can never have enough talking in their lives. Their play and real-world experiences need to be backed up and surrounded with conversation. They need the opportunity to:

- ask questions and have them answered
- express their feelings and ideas and have them taken seriously
- learn new words.

Through their talk with you, and through singing and reciting rhymes, they develop their Communication skills.

? Learning more

You can learn more about your role in providing play and experiences of the real world by taking Unit 2 of the CACHE Diploma in Home-based Childcare.

Planning for progress

Link to ICP
Section 3c

As you get to know the children you care for, you will start to plan ahead the play activities and first-hand experiences to provide for them. You should base your plans on:

- each child's stage of development
  - what can they do?
  - what are they trying to do, what do they almost have the skill to do?
- what interests them, what do they enjoy?

You will find out the answers to these questions if you observe children as they play and engage in other activities. Active observation is about more than just watching children in a general way to check on their safety and well-being. It is about giving them your full attention, looking at them and listening to them carefully. As you observe them in this way, you will learn a lot about how far they have developed, and about what their interests are. This will point you towards the opportunities for play and other experiences you could provide for them to help them progress.

? Learning more

You can learn more about meeting children's learning needs in Unit 5 of the CACHE Diploma in Home-based Childcare.

Each child as an individual

Link to ICP
Sections 6a, 6b

Each child is an individual, different from every other child. Even twins or triplets who may look alike can have differing personalities, skills and abilities. Childcarers sometimes say that they treat 'all children the same', but each child has their own individual needs, so it is sometimes necessary to treat children differently in order to give them all the same opportunities.

5 Planning to work with children

Spotlight on practice

Jamila cares for a 6-year-old boy with physical disabilities which mean that he finds it difficult to sit up unless his back is well supported. She makes sure that he has his foam shapes comfortably in position so he can sit up at the table to play board games with the other children. He needs that extra attention to have the same opportunities as the others to join in and enjoy the games.

Spotlight on practice

Lesley looks after children from African-Caribbean and Asian backgrounds as well as white children. She provides paints and felt-tip pens in a wide range of skin tones so that all the children have an equal opportunity to paint and draw accurate pictures of themselves, their families and one another.

Jamila and Lesley are treating all the children they care for 'with equal concern' so they are all able to get the most out of their play and learning.

You should never fall into the trap of thinking that because a child is like another child in one way, they are also like that child in other ways. Making assumptions about children because of their skin colour, gender, cultural or family background, or a particular disability can get in the way of making sure you treat each child as an individual.

African–Caribbean boys are very physical and run around a lot.

Asian girls are shy and timid.

Children with Down's syndrome are affectionate.

The kids who live on that estate are badly behaved.

If you make assumptions like those shown in the speech bubbles above, you will not be able to care for and nurture each child as an individual. Your picture of them will be focused on only one aspect of their characteristics, and you won't see them as a whole person, different from everyone else.

When you see each child as unique, you will be able to value each child and focus on meeting all their particular needs. And you need to show them and their family that you recognise their individuality. Praise them for who and what they are, and admire the characteristics that make them special and individual – like their skin colour, their hair texture, and their features.

Remember that every child is unique

Stereotyping and prejudice

Link to ICP
Sections 6c, 6d

You will want all the children you care for to have opportunities to develop their potential and make the most of life. There can be two barriers to this, stereotyping and prejudice, and good childcare practice avoids both of these.

Stereotyping can take the form of assuming that because a child is from a particular ethnic or cultural group, or has a disability, or is of either gender, there are only certain things they can do.

If you have expectations of children like those mentioned in the speech bubbles below, you may be (perhaps unconsciously) putting up barriers to children's access to certain sorts of activities and experiences, and so limiting their learning and development. If you tell girls they ought to care for others and help with clearing up, and tell boys they mustn't cry, you are reinforcing stereotypical views of gender roles in society, and not responding to each child's individual personality.

Prejudice occurs when someone holds a negative view about another person because of their gender, ethnic or cultural background, or disability. It usually leads to discrimination – treating a person less favourably than others.

Girls like dressing up and imaginative play, but boys want to be rough or play with trains.

Black boys don't do well at school.

Disabled children can't join in with the outdoor play on the slide and swings.

Disabled children can join in with physical activities

Even small children experience prejudice and discrimination. Many people like to think that young children 'don't notice' differences, but they do. We teach them to recognise the different colours of red, yellow and blue – and they learn to see differences in skin tone too. By three, children recognise differences in gender and skin colour, and by four, many begin to think that male and white people are of more value than female or black people. By five, some children are learning negative views of disabled people.

And children of all ages at times express prejudice and discriminate against others. They express prejudiced attitudes they hear from adults, call other children names, and discriminate by excluding children from play.

Everyone is harmed by prejudice and discrimination. It harms people it is expressed against because they are hurt and offended, and they may be made to feel ashamed, inferior or abnormal so their self esteem and confidence is damaged. People who hold prejudiced views are also harmed because they have a false and distorted view of the world if they think that white, male or able-bodied people are of more value or are superior to black, female or disabled people, or that only a two-parent nuclear family is 'normal'.

Perhaps the most important aspect of your practice in helping children to grow up free of prejudice and discrimination is through the way you behave towards other people. Children learn values and attitudes by copying adults, and if you show that you value people equally, whatever their ethnic or cultural background, gender, or disability, you will be setting a good example for the children.
For instance, one way of showing respect to people is to get names right. You should always make sure that you check how to pronounce and spell a name you are not familiar with, especially if it is from a language other than your own. Never substitute another name just because you find it easier to pronounce.

Key to good practice

One way you can avoid the negative effects of stereotyping and prejudice in your home-based setting is to make sure that children see lots of 'positive images'. This means having pictures, books, puzzles, video tapes and board games which include images of:

- ✔ girls and women shown as strong and independent

- ✔ boys and men shown as emotional, creative and caring

- ✔ disabled children and adults playing active roles, for example, as the 'hero' of a story

- ✔ black people, women and disabled people taking responsible, challenging and influential roles. (It is not difficult to find puzzles and books with black doctors, and female firefighters, but you may have to search and ask for materials which portray disabled people in active roles.)

This helps children to believe that 'the world is their oyster', in other words to develop expectations about their potential to achieve in life, whatever their skin tone, gender or disability.

Including all children

Link to ICP
Section 6e

If you are a childminder, you need to show all children that they 'belong' in your home. If a black child or a disabled child finds no visual representations of black people or disabled people in your setting, it is understandable if they and their family think that your service is not really aimed at people like them, and that they are in some way outsiders. This could have a damaging effect on them, making them feel that they are not as valued by you as the other children you care for. They may not feel secure and comfortable in your setting.

Key to good practice

You can overcome this by using materials that reflect the lives of the children and families who come to your setting, and who are part of your local community:

✓ books and puzzles, dolls, puppets and 'small world' figures which include people:
  • from the ethnic and cultural/religious backgrounds of the children in your setting
  • with disabilities similar to children in the setting
  • from family groupings (such as lone parent, mixed heritage, large extended, same sex parents) like those of the children in the setting

✓ pretend play equipment such as cooking pots and pans, play food, dressing-up clothes and dolls' clothes, and musical instruments used in various cultures so the children can play out their imaginative ideas with what is used and worn in their own families

✓ paint or crayons in relevant skin tones so children are able to portray themselves and their family accurately

✓ books which include the language/script used in the children's homes.

Learning more

You can learn more about:
• inequality, prejudice and discrimination and their effects on children and their families
• equal opportunities and anti-discrimination practice
• challenging prejudice and discrimination
• working with disabled children and their families
in Unit 2 of the CACHE Diploma in Home-based Childcare.

CHAPTER 6

Getting down to business

This chapter will help you with the business aspects of your job.

6 Getting down to business

Whether you are a childminder or a nanny, you need to get the business aspects of your job sorted out. Worries about money matters can be stressful and distract you from focusing your attention on the children and their families. Childminders are self-employed, and nannies are employed, so there are several different issues to be considered, but some – such as insurance – apply to both groups.

This chapter looks at:

- financial matters
- promoting your service
- keeping financial records
- insurance
- policies.

The childminding business

Probably, like many people who choose to become childminders, part of your decision rested on being your own boss. But, of course, that also means you have sole responsibility for the financial aspects of your childminding business, and must get well organised from the beginning.

Getting started financially

Before you can offer a childminding service, you need to buy equipment and materials to start up, and you may need to pay to advertise your new business. Many childminders can get financial support to set up and get initial training.

> ▷ **Take action!**
>
> Contact your local authority, Children's Information Service or NCMA, SCMA or NICMA and ask what start-up business support is available to you.

Making an income

Before you advertise your services and take on the first children, you need to give careful thought to setting the rate you will charge. It is up to you to set your own rates, but you will need to think about:

Link to ICP
Section 8e

- the expenses you are going to encounter in running your childminding business

- how much money you want to be able to take out of the business as regular income for you and your family
- the 'going rate' in your area – what parents are able and willing to pay for the services of a childminder.

▷ Take action!

Begin by making a list of everything you will have to spend money on in order to run your childminding business, and making an estimate of what these will be over the first few weeks and months. And don't forget to keep a record of the start-up costs. Over a period of time you will need to recoup any not covered by start-up support. Find out about tax break arrangements for wear and tear and heating in your home.

Once you have worked out roughly what your business costs are likely to be, you will be in a position to work out a realistic amount to charge parents. You need to add on to those costs an amount which will give you income for the demanding, responsible and challenging work of being a childminder. This will give you a figure for what you need to charge parents.

When you negotiate your charges with parents, don't forget to make clear what payment you expect for:

- absences of the child and illness (child's, parents', yours)
- unsocial hours
- retainers (to keep a place open, for example, during maternity leave).

Possible costs involved in a childminding business:

- play materials such as glue, paper and paints, flour to make dough
- meals and snacks for the children being looked after
- toiletries such as wipes, tissues, extra loo rolls and soap, and first aid supplies
- replacements as equipment wears out – toys, books, childcare equipment (double buggy) and safety equipment (stair-gate, fire blanket)
- insurance (see later in this chapter)
- training courses, including first aid
- membership of NCMA, SCMA or NICMA
- stationery to run your business – account book, contracts, accident book
- phone calls and postage related to childminding
- transport costs – petrol or fares

You also need to think about:

- wear and tear on your home, including cleaning carpets and furniture
- extra heating.

Be sure that both you and the parents understand whether or not your charges include:

- holidays (parents' and yours)
- playgroup/pre-school fees, outings and other extras
- food, nappies etc.

or whether you charge for them separately, and if you make a reduction for more than one child from a family. It is best to include your arrangements for these items in your contract with the parents.

The current childminding rates in your area will depend on local levels of income and the gap between supply and demand for childcare.

Learning more

Northern Ireland CMA publishes a guide, *Negotiating with Parents*.

Encourage parents to claim for the financial help they are entitled to for childcare costs such as Working Tax Credit or vouchers from their employer so they are more able to pay you a reasonable rate.

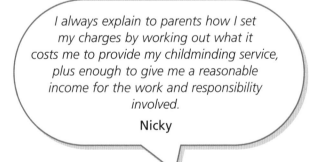

I always explain to parents how I set my charges by working out what it costs me to provide my childminding service, plus enough to give me a reasonable income for the work and responsibility involved.

Nicky

Learning more

NCMA, SCMA and NICMA provide information on all aspects of running your business, so contact them if you need advice on working out your business costs and setting your charges.

Promoting your service

As your registration proceeds and you get nearer to the time when you will be able to open your doors to the first children, you need to think about how to promote your business and find your first customers. Parents can get lists of registered childminders from the local Children's Information Service, but you can't rely on this as a source of business when nurseries and other childcare providers advertise in the press and on radio in this increasingly competitive market. You probably can't afford to spend a lot on expensive advertisements and glossy brochures, but there are some low-cost methods you could use to advertise.

Spotlight on practice

- Jenny has always had a bit of a flair for design and she has made a simple but eye-catching leaflet on her family's home computer. It includes information about the area she lives in (not her exact address), the times she offers her service, her training and experience, the schools and playgroups she can cover – and she makes a big point that she is properly registered, insured and a member of the Scottish Childminding Association (she uses the full name because parents may not know the initials). She sends copies to the personnel departments of local big employers, estate agents, jobcentres, as well as dropping some in to the health centre and library.

A leaflet to promote childminding services

- Barrie uses the postcard sized vacancy cards sold by NCMA. He puts them in newsagents' windows, the local clinic and the leisure centre where ante-natal and post-natal exercise classes are held. He also gives copies to people he thinks will pass on the information by word of mouth – the local National Childbirth Trust and other organisers of ante-natal and post-natal classes, as well as midwives and health visitors.
- Phaitoon uses NCMA vacancy posters on notice boards in the local school, pre-school, community centre, and library.
- Toni's teenage daughter and her friends designed a website for her, as part of a college project. They made sure that it had the right wording so people will find the website when they're searching on the Internet. She put in her phone number and gave her postcode, not her address to avoid unwelcome callers.
- Rick lives on a road where people pass the house regularly and he has a board in the garden.

And don't forget to let other childminders in the area know when you have vacancies – if they're full, they may pass on enquiries to you.

When you're promoting your business, think about what parents want to know when they're making childcare choices. Mention the play activities you offer, any regular places you go such as the park or childminders' drop-in, your first aid qualification, and the nutritious food you provide. Think about your 'unique selling point' (USP) and explain to parents what makes your service special. Describe the advantages of home-based care in offering children a home atmosphere, with individual attention, staying in their own community. Point out the advantages of brothers and sisters coming to the same place for childcare. If you can work irregular or out-of-the-norm hours, emphasise your flexibility. Mention any special experience or skills such as working with disabled children.

Learning more

Contact NCMA, SCMA or NICMA for more information about how to promote your business. You can also learn more about marketing your childminding service in Unit 3 of the CACHE Diploma in Home-based Childcare.

Keeping financial records

Link to ICP
Section 8f

▷ Take action!

As a self-employed person, you must register as soon as possible with HM Revenue and Customs. You will find their details in the Useful contacts section at the end of this book. (There are fines for people who do not register.)

In due course, you will have to complete a self-assessment income tax return. You can do this by filling in a form, or using the customer-friendly system online at www.hmrc.gov.uk. To be ready to complete this self-assessment, you must keep records of your income and expenditure for tax purposes. If you keep your records up-to-date, it will be a great help in filling your annual tax return.

Records of income mainly consist of the amounts parents pay you (start-up grants are not taxable). It is good practice to give them a dated receipt when they pay. This avoids confusion and ensures you have a record of what you were paid and when. It is a good idea to record these payments in a proper accounts book (such as the ones sold by NCMA, SCMA and NICMA) and ask parents to sign to confirm what they have paid you.

However, you will not have to pay tax on the whole amount they pay you, being entitled to deduct your business expenses.

Keep a record too of all the money you spend in connection with your childminding business. Use the list given earlier in this chapter as a starting point, and record these in your accounts book. Get into the habit of doing this regularly – weekly if possible, so you don't forget to note down what you have spent. Keep all receipts and make a note of any that are missing.

? Learning more

NCMA, SCMA and NICMA can provide detailed advice about 'allowable costs' including those for heat, light, water rates, council tax, rent and wear and tear on your home.

When you know your total expenditure for the tax year, you can deduct it from your total childminding income. That will give you your 'net income' which will form the basis for the calculation of your tax bill. You may find that when your tax allowances have been taken into account, you have to pay little or no tax – but you still have to keep financial records and complete a tax return. And you may be eligible for tax credits, especially if you have children of your own. To find out if you qualify, call the tax credits helpline (see the Useful contacts section at the end of this book).

Besides income tax, you need to clarify your position about National Insurance contributions. If you earn very little, you may be able get 'exemption' from payments, but before you decide to do this, you should take into account the likely effects on your state pension and other benefits. Contact the National Insurance self-employed helpline to find out what is best for you (see the Useful contacts section at the end of this book).

It is also possible that, even though you are childminding, you may be able to claim certain benefits – for example housing or council tax benefit – as there are special rules for childminders. You can get a benefits check through your local jobcentre or Citizens' Advice Bureau.

The NCMA accounts book can help you keep your finances straight

? Learning more

The NCMA provides all its members with handbooks explaining all these aspects of running your business in great detail.

The handbooks NCMA provides for members are
full of valuable advice on running your business

▷ Take action!

Make sure you find out whether you can claim another source of income, repayment for the milk or
fruit you give the children. Contact NCMA, SCMA or NICMA to find out about how to claim.

Financial matters for nannies

Nannies and other home-based childcarers working in families' homes are employed by the families they work for, so you have certain rights as an employed person. For example:

- you must be paid at least the minimum wage
- your employer is responsible for your income tax and National Insurance (NI) payments, not you (they may prefer to use a specialist payroll service such as Nannytax to make sure that your tax and National Insurance contributions are dealt with properly)
- they should pay you sick pay if you are off work because of illness
- they must take out employer's liability insurance (in case you have an accident while working in their home)
- you are entitled to annual holiday and time off each week.

The amount you are paid will depend on such things as:

- the hours you work
- whether you live in the family's home or your own
- your experience and qualifications
- the number of children you look after
- the 'going rate' in your part of the country.

You should be paid regularly, and given a pay slip with your wages setting out the tax and NI deductions. Clarify with your employer what expenses you can claim (for example, fares for taking the children out), and agree a way of you keeping a record and receipts so you can claim each week or month.

Finding the right job

There are hundreds of advertisements every week for nannies, primarily in the magazines *Nursery World* or *The Lady*, and you will get an idea of the sort of jobs currently on offer from these. Probably the easiest way to find a job, especially if you are new to nannying, is through a nanny agency. Look for contact details in *Nursery World* or *The Lady*, or on the Internet, or contact the Recruitment and Employment Confederation on 020 7462 3260 or at www.rec.uk.com/sector-groups/childcare for details of reputable agencies in your area. There are a few big agencies that cover the whole of the UK, but most are smaller and cover a particular area, or specialise in, for example, nannies for new babies, or overseas work. It is the parent, not you, who should pay the fee to the agency for matching you to a family.

A good nanny agency will carry out several checks on you before taking you onto their books. They will probably want to see your CV (curriculum vitae – a history of your qualifications and career) and interview you, check your qualifications, references and previous employment, as well as getting a Criminal Records Bureau (CRB) check and a health declaration. They should not pressurise you into taking a job you don't feel is right for you.

Check with your employer what expenses you can claim

Your CV is important as the first step in 'selling' yourself to a prospective employer. Make yours look professional – no more than two sides of A4 paper, set out clearly, including:

- details of the training you have done and the qualifications you have gained (with dates, name of the college and the awarding body)
- previous jobs – the nature of the position (sole charge, ages of children), why you left, with dates
- the skills you feel you bring to the job (including whether you have a driving licence)
- if you have obtained approval, explain what this means and the checks that have been carried out
- the names of two referees.

An agency can help you get a job

It's a good idea to ask someone else to look over what you write to pick up any slips or contradictions. Parents or an agency should check your employment history and qualifications, so be sure to send the CV to them before the interview.

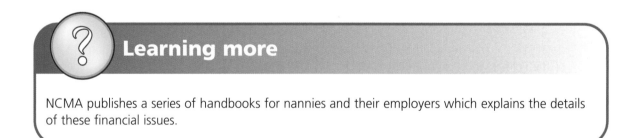

? Learning more

NCMA publishes a series of handbooks for nannies and their employers which explains the details of these financial issues.

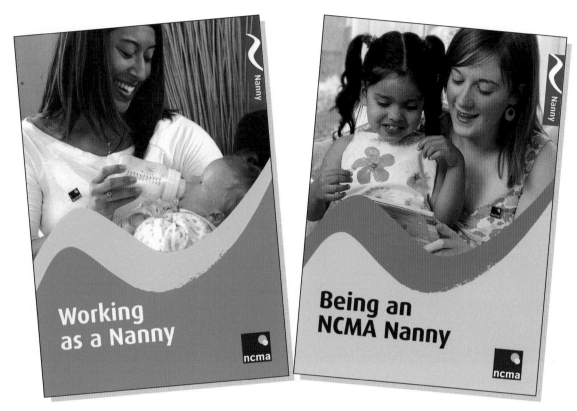

Nanny members of NCMA get advice on financial issues

Insurance

Link to ICP
Section 8h

Insurance is essential for both childminders and nannies. Public liability insurance insures you against liability for accidents to children in your care, or for the damage done to someone else's property by the children in your care. Registered childminders are legally required to have public liability insurance cover, but nannies and other home-based childcarers should also provide themselves with this cover. If you do not, and a child is involved in an accident for which you are to blame, the parents may sue you. This could have grave financial consequences for you and your family.

Childminders should check whether their home contents insurance covers them for childminding, and nannies should make sure that their employers have an 'endorsement' to cover nannies working in their home, in case you accidentally break or damage something that belongs to them.

Find out too the implications for car insurance and make sure that you have 'business' cover. If you don't arrange this, the insurers may refuse to pay any claim you make, or could even cancel or invalidate your policy (which could have very serious possible consequences with car insurance which is required by law).

Make sure you have the right car insurance to cover your childcare work

Drawing up policies

Link to ICP
Section 8g

A policy is a written statement about how you work in one area of your practice. Policies can guide various aspects of your practice, and make clear to parents how you intend to work. Childminders are required to have a variety of written policies. A policy does not have to be a complex document – short, straightforward policies are more likely to be of use. It should communicate clearly in direct language and be well laid out.

? Learning more

If you are hoping to register as a childminder, NCMA can provide mentoring support to you in drawing up your policies. You can learn more about writing policies in Unit 3 of the CACHE Diploma in Home-based Childcare.

CHAPTER 7

Getting started

This chapter will help you make a good start in your relationship with parents and families, and to begin caring for the children.

You need to work well with both the children and their families from the very beginning. This chapter looks at:

- establishing good relationships with parents
- helping children to adjust to new childcare arrangements
- food and mealtimes
- setting a framework for children's behaviour
- looking after children of different ages.

Relationships with parents

Link to ICP
Sections 4a, 4f

It is essential that you establish strong professional relationships with the parents of the children you care for. The way you should work with parents is 'in partnership' – working together to achieve the best for their children. A successful partnership needs good communication and mutual respect.

You need to be able to communicate effectively with parents about all aspects of their children's welfare and development so that you and they, together, can ensure the best for each child. If there is tension and misunderstanding between you, information may not get passed to and fro properly, and this may prevent you meeting the children's needs fully. Children pick up on adults' poor relationships and become confused and unhappy if the grown-ups who matter to them don't seem to be getting on. You should make every effort to make time to talk with parents as much as possible, and be open, honest and cordial in the way you communicate with them.

Meeting parents

Link to ICP
Section 4f

You want to start your relationship with parents in a positive way, but it is understandable if you feel nervous before you meet them for the first time. If you are a nanny, you will probably meet parents through a fairly formal interview, and for childminders, the first meeting with new parents is almost like an interview – with each side interviewing the other! Whether you are a nanny going for an interview in a family's home, or a childminder being visited in your own home, you may feel that you are being put under the microscope and that may make you feel uncomfortable. But remember, the parents are likely to be feeling just as apprehensive as you are about meeting a new person.

Think about it!

Plan ahead for this first meeting. Start by thinking about:

- how parents feel about the prospect of leaving their child with you
- what they want to know about the service you can offer.

This will help you to provide them with information and respond to their questions.

How parents feel

Parents often approach finding childcare with a range of complex feelings. They miss their child, and may feel sad about having to leave them with someone else. Some may feel guilty because they can't spend more time with their child, and a few may even become a bit jealous of the time you spend with their child and the relationship you develop with them.

Respecting parents' choices

Being a childcarer is not a job for someone who 'doesn't really approve of mothers who go out to work'. Mothers choose to work outside the home for many reasons. Their family's finances may require the income, they may need to sustain their career, or they may want stimulation or company for themselves. If you appeared to disapprove of their choice, it would affect the quality of your relationship. And, remember, most childminders are 'working mothers' too.

What parents want to know

Parents need a lot of detailed information before they make the decision to entrust their child to your care. Many first-time parents may feel uncertain about how to judge whether you are a suitable person to look after their child, and may not have the knowledge and experience to ask the right questions to find out all they need to know. You can help them feel confident about the way you will care for their precious child by supplying information about the childcare service you can offer.

Link to ICP
Section 4b

Make sure you explain to parents:

✓ how you plan for the children to spend their day – play activities, meals, going out, television, stories, naps

✓ your approach to:

- bringing up children – for example, setting limits to behaviour, equal opportunities for all children
- safety (including, if the children are to be taken in a car, using restraints) and how you would deal with an emergency
- providing food (including snacks and sweets)

✓ your experience and training in looking after other people's children

✓ details of your registration or approval and insurance

✓ the hours and days you can offer your service, and your availability for taking children to and from playgroup/pre-school and school

✓ how much you expect to be paid.

If you are a childminder, explain:

✓ which rooms (and garden) you will be using – and show them around

✓ how many other children are being minded, and their ages

✓ about members of your family

✓ what sort of pets you keep and children's access to them

✓ that you cannot care for children who are ill

✓ about smoking in your home.

You may be able to provide some of this information in writing in advance of the first meeting. If you are a childminder, you could put quite a lot of it into a simple leaflet; if you are a nanny, send your CV.

Lend useful publications to parents to help them ask you the right questions

It can be useful to keep a copy of either NCMA's *Choosing a Home Childcarer* or Sure Start's *Employing an Approved Childcarer* – and lend it to parents so they can think about some of the questions they need to clarify with you.

As you become established, you may be able to build up a 'portfolio' to show new parents. Include your registration or approval and insurance certificates, your training and qualifications certificates, testimonials from other parents, photographs of the activities you do with children (be sure to get parents' permission to do this), and, if you are a childminder, your last inspection report.

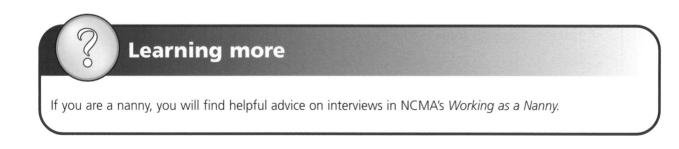

? Learning more

If you are a nanny, you will find helpful advice on interviews in NCMA's *Working as a Nanny.*

7 Getting started

What you need to know

To look after a child, you need to get to know them well, and the information parents give you is the basis of this.

Link to ICP
Section 8b

Key to good practice

Make sure you find out about:

✓ other members of the child's family (including pets)

✓ any special words, names and other vocabulary specific to the child, and what language is spoken at home

✓ any special object or toy that the child finds a comfort

✓ what the child does and does not like to eat; what parents want and do not want the child to eat

✓ anything the child finds alarming or unsettling (for example, dogs, people in spectacles)

✓ any aspects of the family's cultural, religious or traditional background that have implications for caring for their child

✓ the parents' attitude to the activities you plan for the children, including taking them out (to shops, park, drop-in, etc.)

✓ whether the child uses a cup and specific eating implements

✓ information about nappies and/or toilet training

✓ whether the child still has a nap and any routines which help the child to sleep

✓ whether the child has any allergies, health problems or impairments, and what immunisations they have had

✓ any new factors or special problems in the child's life.

You also need to have a written record of:

✓ where parents can be contacted in an emergency – address and phone number

✓ details of the child's doctor and health visitor.

Childminders also need to know who will be collecting the child and if there is anyone who is not permitted contact with the child.

You may not meet the children at the first encounter with the parents, and it is important that you do this before finally agreeing to care for a child.

CHILD RECORD FORM
To be completed and signed by the parent/guardian/carer and given to the childminder.
Please read notes for guidance on the inside front cover of this pad.

ncma

Child's name (1) _____ Date of birth_____

Home address _____

_____ Telephone number_____

DETAILS OF PARENTS/GUARDIANS/CARERS

Parent's/Guardian's/Carer's Name_____

Address (if different from above) _____

Place of work_____ Work number_____ Mobile_____

Parent's/Guardian's/Carer's Name_____

Address (if different from above) _____

Place of work_____ Work number_____ Mobile_____

Emergency contact (other than parent/guardian/carer) _____

Name of person who usually collects the child (2) _____

Other person(s) who may collect the child _____ Password_____

Other person(s) who may collect the child _____ Password_____

Further information (if necessary) _____

CHILD'S DOCTOR

Name and Address _____

_____ Telephone Number_____

Immunisations/Vaccinations Has the child been fully immunised against:

Diphtheria ☐ Whooping Cough ☐ Tetanus ☐ Polio ☐ Measles ☐ Mumps ☐ Rubella ☐ Hib Meningitis ☐

Health clinic _____

Health visitor _____

Allergies/ Special diet/ Health problems/ Childhood illnesses (3) _____

_____

_____

Language spoken at home (4) _____ Child's religion/culture_____

Anything else your childminder should know about your child e.g. likes, dislikes, fears, comfort items, special words (5)

_____

_____

_____

Parents should notify the childminder of any changes to these details immediately. Details of any accidents which occur while the child is in the care of the childminder should be recorded in the Accident, Incident and Medication Record Book and signed by the parent/guardian/carer.

National Childminding Association
Royal Court, 81 Tweedy Road, Bromley, Kent BR1 1TG
Telephone: 0845 880 0044 Fax: 0845 880 0043

Parent/Guardian/Carer (6)
Signature _____ Date _____

© National Childminding Association

NCMA's record forms help you to keep written information about children in your care (© NCMA)

Contracts

Link to ICP
Section 8c

Having a written contract with parents forms a sound basis for a good relationship. It gives you a chance to set out clearly the details of the arrangements you make with them. Nannies are employees so must, by law, have a written contract within eight weeks of starting work (though NCMA recommends that a contract is agreed from the time the nanny starts work). For childminders, having a written contract creates a business-like relationship – and that gives parents confidence that you are well organised. Above all, having things in writing helps to prevent misunderstandings from developing. Without a written contract, there is no legal arrangement and no way of showing what was agreed if the arrangements break down at a later date. Even if you are only agreeing short-term arrangements, or if the parents are friends or family members, you should have a written agreement.

NCMA's *Working as a Nanny* and Sure Start's *Employing an Approved Childcarer* set out in detail what should be in a nanny's contract. And NCMA, SCMA and NICMA publish contract forms for childminders that have been tried and tested as legal documents and will help you to make sure that you include all aspects which are important.

Key to good practice

Here are some suggestions to help you get the contract relationship off on a firm footing:

✓ When you start discussing whether or not you will look after a child, tell the parents that you expect there to be written, signed contracts to help keep arrangements clear.

✓ If you are a nanny, point out the section in 'Employing an Approved Childcarer' which talks about contracts; if you are a childminder, lend the parent a copy of the NCMA model contract to read through.

✓ Go through the contract carefully together, and clarify all the details about:

- the days and times the parent will need your service
- payment – when you will be paid, any variations for overtime and unsocial hours, and holiday pay
- illness (child's, parents', yours)
- giving notice or payment in lieu.

Childminders should also clarify:

- the meals you will be responsible for providing
- what parents will provide or pay extra for (nappies, special foods, change of clothes) and payments for playgroup/pre-school, outings
- if it's relevant, talk about charges for more than one child from a family (some childminders give a reduction)
- a settling-in period of 3–4 weeks before the contract comes into operation, to make sure the arrangements work out

Nannies should also clarify:

- expectations about duties
- accommodation
- use of the car
- arrangements about having visitors, use of the family's phone, etc.

✓ Be prepared to negotiate some aspects of the contract to fit in with parents' needs, but be firm about the ones you feel you must stick to.

✓ Make sure you both sign **and date** the contract and keep a copy each.

✓ Make a note on your calendar of when the review of the contract and payment rates is due and remember to remind the parent that it's coming.

✓ Tell the parents about NCMA's information line (see the Useful contacts section at the end of this book) and explain that it is available to parents as well as childminders and nannies.

Childminders will find that families often have different requirements for each of their children, so you need a separate contract for each child.

Remember that a contract works both ways – the parent is undertaking to pay you as agreed, and you are undertaking to provide the service described. You must keep your side of the contract too.

Discuss all the details of your contract with parents

Take action!

NCMA provides a wealth of information and advice on contracts. *Running your Childminding Business* or *Working as a Nanny* are essential reading to help you make sure that the contract you sign and bind yourself to legally is one that will either help you run an effective business as a childminder or protect your rights as an employed nanny.

Helping children to adjust

Link to ICP
Sections 4c, 4d, 4e

When you first start caring for children, you have to make sure that you help them adjust to the new situation – of coming to your home if you are a childminder, or having you in their home if you are a nanny. Some children find it difficult to cope with being separated from the familiar adults in their lives. This depends partly on their stage of development. For example, new babies seem to be OK about being cared for by various adults, but as they approach the age of one they may experience 'stranger anxiety' – they are wary of people they don't know. Many under threes feel 'separation anxiety' – they are unhappy about being separated from their known adults.

You need to give a child time to adjust at a pace that's realistic for that child at that stage of development. Some parents feel it reflects badly on them if their child seems 'clingy'. I try to get across to them that I expect that it will take a while for the child to settle and begin to feel relaxed with me and come to trust me as one of their special grown-ups.

Zoe

Key to good practice

Give lots of individual attention to the child while they're getting used to being with you. Let them be the centre of your attention in the early days. All the information the parents have given you about their child will help you to begin to relate to that child and understand their particular characteristics, likes and dislikes.

If you are a childminder, provide a warm welcome to your home. Take time to show a new child around your house and garden, explaining about where they will spend time and the sort of things you will be doing together. Introduce them to each of the other children and members of your own family (don't forget your pets). Don't hurry any of this, and explain everything. Plan ahead so you can avoid more than one new child starting with you at the same time.

Give children a lot of your attention to help them settle

There are various strategies you can use to help children get used to being with you.

Spotlight on practice

Phil is a childminder, and he arranges for a new child to visit his home with a parent first of all, and then move on to short stays with him alone, and then when some of the other children and members of his family are around.

Spotlight on practice

Ros is also a childminder and she asks parents to leave something belonging to them – like a scarf or glove. She finds this helps to reassure the child that mum or dad will be back to collect them both – glove and child.

> I think it's important for children to bring their 'cuddly' with them – it gives them a link with home.
>
> **Aneesh**

> I encourage parents to say goodbye properly and then go, not hanging about. I think if they try to 'sneak out' when they leave it makes a child feel abandoned and betrayed. The child and I wave goodbye out of the window, and then we have a story or play together, usually with a good cuddle.
>
> **Clare**

> I play a tape of the parents' voices talking and singing to help babies settle happily.
>
> **Denise**

Parents may be concerned or even embarrassed if their child cries when they leave. Reassure them that it is perfectly normal for young children to find separation difficult. Some children have a temporary setback in their development, and go back to thumb sucking or wetting themselves. Make it clear that you don't think the child is babyish. In fact, you might be concerned about the emotional development of a child who was completely unconcerned about being separated from their parents!

It's better to say 'goodbye' properly

Providing the service parents want

Link to ICP
Sections 2a, 4f

All families have different ways of bringing up their children, based on their values and way of life which may reflect their cultural or social background. An important aspect of your partnership relationship with parents is to listen to and respect their views and ways of doing things, and to discuss with them how far you can provide what they want for their child. Examples of this may be about:

- food and mealtimes
- managing children's behaviour.

Food and mealtimes

Some parents will have particular requirements and requests about their children's diet.

- Some children have allergies to certain foods, or cannot tolerate additives. Some allergies, such as nuts (especially peanuts), can be dangerous or even potentially fatal, so you must follow what the parents tell you.

- Some families follow a particular diet for reasons connected with their religious or other beliefs. Don't fall into the trap of assuming that because a child belongs to a specific cultural or religious group, their family sticks rigidly to the diet associated with it.

> *I would never agree to provide a certain kind of diet and then ignore parents' requirements and wishes. That isn't respectful to parents and it's not right for children.*
>
> **Annette**

If you don't feel confident about meeting parents' requests, ask them to give you advice on preparing meals for their child.

Children need a balanced diet, with all the nutrients – protein, fibre, calcium, minerals, vitamins – so it's important that you agree with parents what food (meals and snacks) you will give their children so that, between you, you meet all their nutritional needs, and avoid too much fat, salt, sugar and additives.

? Learning more

You can learn more about diet and nutrition by taking Unit 2 of the CACHE Diploma in Home-based Childcare.

Some parents will be keen for you to encourage good 'table manners'. Rigid table manners can be very challenging for young children, but learning adult eating habits will make children more welcome at meal tables. Make sure you tune in to the variety of families' manners, derived from cultural, religious or traditional practices, and find out whether the child's family:

- sits at a table or on the floor
- uses knives and forks or chopsticks or fingers.

Parents may be concerned about their children's eating 'fads'. Tackle this by:

- making food attractive
- letting children eat what they can and will

Find out about family mealtimes

- introducing children to a wide variety of tastes, whilst respecting their right not to have to eat things they really don't like (adults don't)
- not letting battles develop over food – spending a lot of time and energy on persuading a child to eat teaches them that refusing food is a good way to get attention.

You may find that children who are 'fussy eaters' with their parents will try the new foods that you give them.

A framework for children's behaviour

Link to ICP
Section 5c

As a professional childcarer, you need to set a 'framework' for the behaviour of the children you care for. Begin with deciding what sort of behaviour will and will not be acceptable in your home-based childcare setting, your 'house rules', and then go on to thinking about how you will encourage children to live up to your expectations. It is important to discuss this framework with parents before you start caring for their child so you can agree a shared approach.

It is positive and helpful to children to make clear to them what the boundaries or limits are for the way they behave. It can be very reassuring to them because they know where they are, how far they can go.

Your 'rules' are likely to be based on guiding children away from doing things that:

- are dangerous, hurtful or offensive to others (other children, adults)
- are a danger to the children themselves
- will make the child unwelcome or unacceptable to other people
- damage other people's belongings.

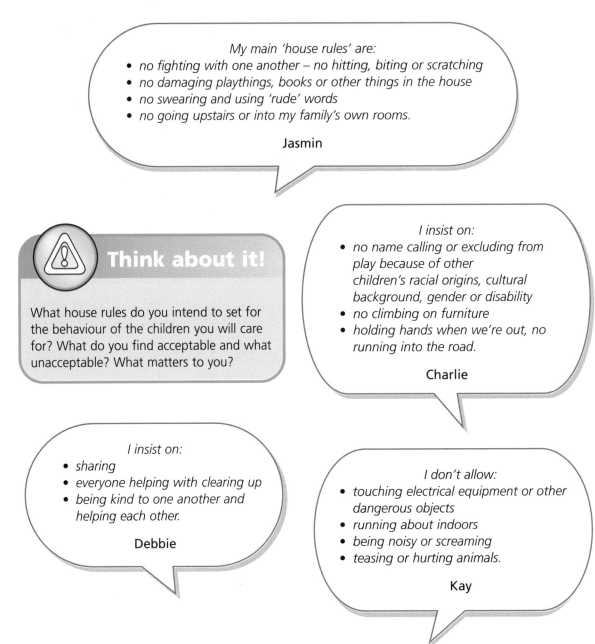

My main 'house rules' are:
- *no fighting with one another – no hitting, biting or scratching*
- *no damaging playthings, books or other things in the house*
- *no swearing and using 'rude' words*
- *no going upstairs or into my family's own rooms.*

Jasmin

Think about it!

What house rules do you intend to set for the behaviour of the children you will care for? What do you find acceptable and what unacceptable? What matters to you?

I insist on:
- *no name calling or excluding from play because of other children's racial origins, cultural background, gender or disability*
- *no climbing on furniture*
- *holding hands when we're out, no running into the road.*

Charlie

I insist on:
- *sharing*
- *everyone helping with clearing up*
- *being kind to one another and helping each other.*

Debbie

I don't allow:
- *touching electrical equipment or other dangerous objects*
- *running about indoors*
- *being noisy or screaming*
- *teasing or hurting animals.*

Kay

'Rules' are often expressed in a negative way, so children find themselves in the situation of being told constantly by adults what they shouldn't or mustn't do, but they are not clear about what adults *do* want them to do. Try to express as many of your 'rules' as possible in a positive way, as 'expectations'. Take the positive approach of explaining clearly to children what you expect of them and how you *do* want them to behave, then they know what to aim for.

Explain your expectations for behaviour

Key to good practice

✓ Don't set expectations which children can't really understand yet because they won't be able to live up to them. For example, it may be unreasonable to expect all toddlers to share or all under sevens to take turns.

✓ Be fair – for example, set similar expectations of behaviour for both boys and girls: don't let boys be rough, but not girls.

✓ Talk with parents about why you set certain expectations, and find out what the child has learned about acceptable behaviour so far.

✓ Remember that children from some social and cultural groupings will have learned different rules about what is and is not acceptable behaviour. For example:

- in some traditions it is not considered polite for a child to look an adult straight in the eyes
- in some social groups, it is not 'the done thing' to express strong emotions
- in some cultures, saying 'please' and 'thank you' is less important than in others.

✓ If you are a childminder, you will need to give some thought to whether you have the same expectations and rules for your own children.

Encouraging positive behaviour

There are several possible 'strategies' for guiding the way children behave in a positive way and helping them to live up to your expectations for their behaviour. On the whole, children want to please the adults who are important to them.

Link to ICP
Section 5c

Key to good practice

✓ When children behave well, show your approval with rewards like:
- hugs and smiles
- approving words and praise
- your attention and time to talk and play (children become 'attention seeking' when they aren't given attention).

✓ Make sure you tell their parents and other people when they have behaved well.

✓ Explain why certain kinds of behaviour are expected. ('It's dangerous, it will hurt.')

✓ Don't create confrontations. Don't over-react or make a big deal over minor matters – avoid battles.

✓ Be firm: make it clear that you won't surrender to whining or tantrums.

✓ Be consistent: apply the same expectations from one day to the next.

✓ Set a good example: be kind and gentle, considerate and polite; don't shout. Children learn how to behave by copying adults.

Give your attention and time as a reward for 'good' behaviour

Working with children across a wide age range

Home-based childcarers work with a wider age range than other childcare workers, from new babies up into the teens for some children. It can be very rewarding to provide long-term care for a child from the time they are a baby up to and after the time they start school. You may become a trusted close friend of the family, watch the baby grow into a toddler and play a key part in the child's development. Parents often choose home-based childcare because they want this continuity for their child.

It can be very wearing when a baby:

- is 'colicky' and cries and cries
- is miserable because they're teething
- takes a lot of time to feed.

And looking after a baby means:

- having to take nappies, bottle, etc. wherever you go
- practising extra hygiene and extra safety routines (like sterilising bottles and spoons; avoiding putting baby relax seats on tables).

Toddlers can test your patience by:

- touching and damaging things that aren't kept out of their reach (because they want to explore and learn about their surroundings)
- needing close supervision to protect their safety
- their messiness at mealtimes.

Babies and toddlers

Most of us find babies delightful, and we love it when they smile and gurgle at us. We become fascinated with the rapid progress of toddlers. But under twos can be very demanding of time and energy.

Babies can be charming and delightful

Many parents prefer their babies and toddlers to be with a home-based childcarer rather than in group care. They value the close contact with their childminder or nanny and the opportunity to share the care of their very young children with a particular person they can get to know and trust. They feel their baby gets individual, consistent care from the same adult each day and week, something which is not always possible in nurseries, even those which operate a key worker system.

> *I'm not keen on working with babies or toddlers. Babies' routines are very time-consuming and too much of a tie. I don't think I have a calm enough temperament to provide the best care for under twos.*
>
> Penny

Think about it!

There are several factors to bear in mind when you provide care for a baby.

- Breastfeeding mothers will need your support – you may be able to store breast milk and bottle feed it to the baby and/or perhaps the mother can pop in during the day to feed her baby.

- You will need to work very closely with parents to get a consistent approach to weaning and potty training.

- If they can't get time off work, parents may ask you to take the baby to the clinic to be weighed or for their immunisations (be sure to have parents' written permission).

- Most parents will prefer you not to mention if you spot important stages of development – they prefer to be the first to observe the first step, the first tooth for themselves, but check that this really is what the parents want.

Babies' brains double in weight in the first two years of life and research shows that stimulation is essential during that time to help the brain develop. They need to be given chances to use their senses to find out about the world around them – to look, touch, taste, listen, smell. They should have interesting things to watch, sounds to hear, shapes to handle. Babies are ready for social interaction from birth, and stare intently at human faces as they are held and smiled at. Language development begins in a baby's earliest months. They need to hear and develop understanding of language long before they can utter their first words.

Key to good practice

✓ Put up mobiles within their range of vision, and offer them brightly coloured objects.

✓ Help them look in mirrors.

✓ Give them things like rattles and bells which make various noises.

✓ Give them lots of physical contact – stroking, cuddling, tickling.

✓ Make eye contact and play 'peek-a-boo' games.

✓ Talk to them, telling them about what is going on around them.

✓ Play handing to-and-fro games, setting the pattern of the to-and-fro of conversation. Smile at them and return the conversational, 'talking' sounds they make to you.

✓ Play clapping and bouncing games, singing and chanting rhymes.

Babies don't need a lot of elaborate manufactured toys – make them a treasure basket.

As babies move from the sitting up stage to the crawling and walking stages, they go through phases of:

- playing alone (solitary play)
- playing alongside other children (parallel play)
- playing with other children (co-operative play).

Babies enjoy the company of other babies, and even when they're at the solitary play stage, they exchange glances and gestures (such as patting) with other children.

Toddlers need the opportunity to explore their environment, to discover, to try things out and experiment.

Key to good practice

Provide them with:

✓ stacking beakers

✓ bricks

✓ hammer and pegs

✓ posting boxes

✓ simple puzzles

✓ push-and-pull along toys, to encourage mobility

✓ stubby crayons and sheets of paper for them to make marks – their very first attempts at drawing and writing

✓ dolls, puppets and soft toys (a few – don't overdo it!), which can become friends who can have stories made up about them and become part of make-believe play.

Looking at the world through children's eyes

Singing and reciting nursery rhymes is an important part of children's earliest learning, as well as being fun. And it's never too early to introduce books – reading stories, examining the pictures and showing how to turn over pages.

Above all, talk with children as their early language skills emerge.

✓ Talk about everything and anything – what you see when you go out, what you are going to do next, the weather – and name the objects that are part of every day life.

✓ Respond positively to their efforts to speak and if they make mistakes, don't tell them they're getting it wrong, just repeat what they have tried to say correctly.

✓ Give them time to think about and finish what they want to say – don't interrupt or finish their sentences for them.

Because you and the parents know the child so well, you can understand their early attempts at speech, and 'interpret' them to the rest of the world.

Young children don't need huge supplies of bought toys. I have found I can adapt and improvise ordinary things in the house. A cardboard box with a slit in it and some junk mail (we've got plenty of that!) was a great hit. And I've got a little basket with pegs clipped around the rim and a Smarties tube with some pebbles to push through it which have provided hours of entertainment. And, of course, saucepans and wooden spoons are always a surefire hit.

Morag

I love going out with the littlest ones, and looking at the world from their point of view. What can beat walking through scrunchy leaves or blowing dandelion clocks? We spend hours looking under stones for worms and mini-beasts and finding spiders in their webs. It is so wonderful to look at the world afresh – I think I enjoy it as much as they do.

Rhian

School-age children

Think about it!

Your role with children who spend most of term-time days in school is likely to be different from that with younger children. It might include:

- taking them to and from school
- taking them to early evening activities
- listening to them reading and helping them to get their homework done
- looking after them throughout the day in school holidays.

You need to plan so you can fit this into your routines. It can be very worrying for a child, especially in the first few weeks when they start school, if you aren't there promptly at the end of the school day to collect them. So make sure you include enough time in your schedule.

You may not be looking after a child for very long after school, and it would be easy to just let them drift and fill in time before their parents returned. However, to provide a professional service you should offer a variety of purposeful activities, but remember that they've been in a structured environment all day at school, so make activities relaxed and give them freedom of choice.

Competitive activities can encourage some children to stretch themselves and reach their potential, but for many other children the fear of being seen to lose or fail can damage their self-confidence. Co-operative games encourage everyone to join in and enjoy themselves – there are no winners and losers.

> *You have to tune in to what the individual child wants at the end of the school day. Some children come out of school full of energy – they need lots of action. Others are tired and just want to flop on the sofa. I make sure I have some play activities sorted out for them, as well as a snack and a drink – but I also make sure they can do restful things like watching television, if they want to.*
>
> **Tessa**

> *Even after starting school, I found the children went on enjoying the play activities I provided for them when they were younger. They still love to mess about with glue and scrap materials, and I try to think of 'props' for their imaginative play – they seem to be very into being teacher at the moment.*
>
> **Stuart**

> *I think it's fine for the children to watch television after a long and tiring day at school, as long as it's rationed. I vet what they watch and make sure the programmes are suitable, and I try to find the time to watch some with them and have a chat about what they've seen.*
>
> **Elena**

> *I let the children use the computer, but I'm very careful to supervise what they get access to.*
>
> **Gina**

Homework assignments may need the use of a computer

Parents may ask you to take their children to early evening activities, such as swimming or music classes. You will have to think about fitting all this together with homework and quiet times after school, and (if you're a childminder) the times other children are collected by their parents, and the requirements of your own family and personal life. Be realistic about how much can be fitted into this busy time of day – it's likely to be a time when your own energy levels are running low.

If you do agree to take children to an activity, clarify:

- whether you or the parents will collect them (and make sure the person in charge of the activity knows too)
- how any payments are made and by whom.

School holidays will have a big effect on your routines. Younger children are used to being with you most of every day, but the school-age children aren't. They could easily get bored and miserable and disrupt the routine of the younger children. Plan ahead so there are plenty of things to do and you have made any necessary preparations.

Spotlight on practice

Paula is a childminder. Once a week in school holidays she gets together with two other childminders in her area and they take all the minded children, and their own, to a gym session at the local sports centre. The local childminding group usually organises an outing during each school holiday. The most recent was to a city farm, but they've also been on a train ride and had a day on the beach.

Spotlight on practice

Sarah is a nanny who looks after two pre-school children and 9-year-old James. He joins a holiday play scheme for a week during each school holiday. She tries to organise the usual play activities for the rest of the time round a theme that interests James. Sarah and the children:

- read stories and look at books
- make collages from scrap materials and paint
- learn new songs
- dress up in costumes
- cook dishes

all linked to the theme.

The Christmas break provides lots of ideas, but at other times she has done things related to the seasons and weather, or boats (James's real passion). He loves to get involved in:

- planning what to do and when to do it
- finding out information – in the library, on the Internet
- getting materials ready
- recording what goes on – drawing pictures and taking photos, and writing about it all – to share with the rest of the family.

As children grow and develop, they need to start becoming more independent. Restrictions which may be totally reasonable for a 5-year-old may be too restricting for an 8-year-old, and quite smothering for a 10-year-old. You have to find a balance between keeping children safe and letting them learn to take responsibility for themselves.

You must discuss and agree with parents how much freedom you can reasonably give a child so they can develop their independence and their own social circle. Together, you should decide when an individual child is ready to be allowed to play outside the garden, or ride their bike round the block, or pop down to the shop on the corner or to the post box to post a letter.

When agreeing with parents how much freedom a child can have, think about:

- the age and maturity of the child, and their individual personality
- the environment, for example if you're near a busy main road
- the weather and season – you may have different rules for light summer evenings and dark winter afternoons.

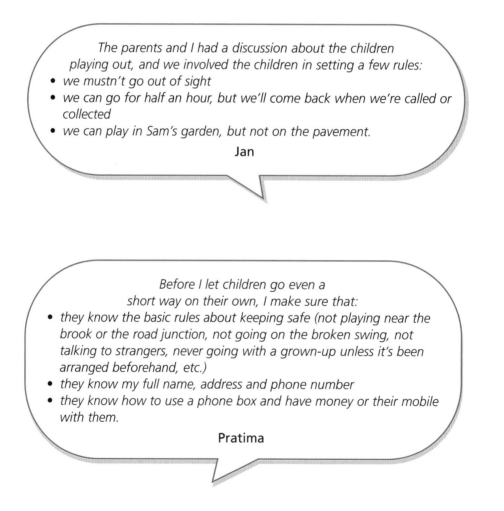

The parents and I had a discussion about the children playing out, and we involved the children in setting a few rules:
- *we mustn't go out of sight*
- *we can go for half an hour, but we'll come back when we're called or collected*
- *we can play in Sam's garden, but not on the pavement.*

Jan

Before I let children go even a short way on their own, I make sure that:
- *they know the basic rules about keeping safe (not playing near the brook or the road junction, not going on the broken swing, not talking to strangers, never going with a grown-up unless it's been arranged beforehand, etc.)*
- *they know my full name, address and phone number*
- *they know how to use a phone box and have money or their mobile with them.*

Pratima

You and the parents should also discuss and agree whether a child should travel to and from school on their own, or whether you will always take and fetch them. Think about:

- the nature of the journey involved – how far, busy roads, isolated paths, roads to be crossed, how much traffic
- how they're going to make the journey – school bus, bike, car
- whether they can have company and walk with a group of friends
- the maturity and reliability of the child.

As they get older, some children don't want to be seen walking with their childminder or nanny and the younger children. The older they get, the less they like it. Try simple rules like agreeing how far ahead they can walk on and wait (to the corner, the post box, the poster with the picture of a tiger). This can help to develop their independence in a safe way, with the added bonus of making a potentially boring routine more interesting – even a learning activity.

Allow leeway for independence

Mixed age groups

If you care for children within a wide age range you will probably find that sometimes the needs and rights of one age group conflict with those of another. You can find yourself constantly juggling to ensure that the routines of the younger children don't take precedence over the needs of older ones – and vice versa. Babies' demands are often inflexible – they can't wait. You have to plan ahead all the time to be ready to respond to the baby, but making sure that the needs of the other children are met too.

> *It can be great looking after a baby and older children at the same time. The baby learns a lot by copying the older children, and the older children benefit from learning how to care for and consider other people. They help the baby and they realise that sometimes they have to wait until I've finished attending to him. But they can get jealous of the amount of my time and attention he uses up, and I feel they have a right to time and attention too. I'm careful not to expect them to always be helping me look after him.*
>
> Laura

Some older children enjoy helping with the little ones

? Learning more

You can learn more about working with children of all ages by taking Unit 2 of the CACHE Diploma in Home-based Childcare.

CHAPTER 8

Keeping it going

This chapter will help you maintain your good start as a home-based childcarer and adopt other aspects of good practice.

8 Keeping it going

Once you get established in your work as a home childcarer, you will begin to focus on other aspects of good practice. This chapter looks at:

- developing your relationship with parents
- confidentiality
- responding to children's challenging behaviour
- children's illness.

Developing your relationship with parents

There are two aspects in developing relationships – exchanging information and maintaining two-way communication.

Exchanging information with parents

We saw in the last chapter how important it is to exchange information with parents when you first start caring for their child. This information exchange goes on being important in your partnership with parents, so together, you can make sure that children get the continuity of care that is essential for their welfare and development.

Link to ICP
Section 4b

🔍 **Key to good practice**

You and each child's parents need to exchange information regularly about such matters as:

✓ what the child has been doing: if the child has been enjoying a play activity, or you have seen something interesting or read a special book together, describe it to the parents so they can go on talking about it and adding to the child's enjoyment and learning

✓ any unusual occurrences: if something upsetting has happened to the child, you and the parents need to tell one another so you can make sure the child is comforted or reassured – or if it was something exciting, you can share the child's pleasure

✓ what the child has eaten and when: this will help you make sure their diet is balanced, and know if a child loses their appetite which could mean they are unwell

▶

✓ nappy/toilet routines: too many or too few dirty nappies or trips to the toilet could also suggest an on-coming illness

✓ sleep and rest patterns: so each of you understands the child's needs for the rest of the day

✓ any concerns: if a child suddenly begins behaving in a way which isn't usual for them, you or the parents should make sure the other party knows about it – it could be a sign of something important which you need to do something about together.

Think about it!

You need to find ways of exchanging information with parents in ways and at times that suit you both. A good approach is to have:

• at least a few minutes daily for a brief exchange of vital information
• a longer proper discussion, perhaps once a week, preferably out of ear-shot of the child.

It isn't always easy to fit in a daily exchange of information – both parents and childcarers have full and busy lives – but you and parents should make every effort to do so for the children's sake.

Spotlight on practice

Sheila is a childminder who uses a daily note book for each child which goes to and from home with them. She notes information that she thinks the parents ought to know as it crops up through the day, and the parents make similar notes at home about what they want to pass on to her. It sometimes signals to them that they need a longer chat to sort something out together.

It is essential to exchange information regularly with parents

Communicating with parents

For your communication with parents to be effective, it must be open and honest, friendly and pleasant. You need to respect one another's ideas and opinions and discuss matters relating to their children in a relaxed and comfortable way. Remember that although you become a very significant person in a child's life, you are never a substitute for parents. Some parents worry that their childminder or nanny will in some way become more important to their child than they are and you need to reassure them that your role is to complement and support the parents' role.

Link to ICP
Section 4f

I try to make it clear to parents that I think that they are the most important people in their child's life. I say that I will play my part in looking after their child, but I can never take the place of a parent, and I would never try to do so.

Andrea

Key to good practice

Sometimes parents may seek your advice about such matters as childhood illnesses and immunisation. You can give them support, but you have to take care not to appear to be too much of an expert. As someone experienced in working with children, there is always the danger that, without meaning to, you could undermine parents' confidence in their parenting skills. This requires tact and sensitivity on your part.

You have to keep a balance between your friendly relationship and the business and professional side of your relationship. If you are a childminder, parents come into your home frequently, and if you are a nanny, you spend a great deal of time in their home. This can make it difficult for home-based childcarers to keep relationships with parents on a professional footing – business-like, within a friendly atmosphere. There is a difference between being friendly and becoming friends.

Think about it!

Give careful thought to how far you want to socialise with the parents of the children you care for. If you get too close, it can be difficult to maintain the business side of the relationship.

Negotiating and agreeing a written and signed contract helps you to make the business aspects of arrangements clear. Regular reviews of your contract are essential, to make adjustments – to hours, rates of pay, etc. The review date should be written into the contract – and make sure you don't let it pass by!

If you are a childminder, when it comes to the time for review you may decide that you have to increase your fees, because your expenses have risen.

I'm always open with parents about how I work out my childminding expenses, so they can see that in fact only part of what they pay me is really my income – the rest goes straight out again on running my childminding business.

Miriam

Both childminders and nannies can make the case for your own need for the same pay rises as parents get in line with the cost of living.

When you were planning to become a home-based childcarer, you took some decisions about the nature of the service you would offer, such as the times you were prepared to work and the ages of the children you felt you wanted to look after. Once you have taken these decisions, you should think carefully before changing your mind. One of the things parents value about home-based childcare is flexibility, and sometimes you will be happy to adjust arrangements to suit a family's changing needs. However, some parents may try to persuade you to make different arrangements which you know you cannot really manage, and you may find it very difficult to resist their requests. You may find yourself under subtle pressures to offer more to the family than you intended, in the name of friendship rather than a business arrangement.

If you ever find yourself in a situation where you just don't feel comfortable in your relationship either with parents or a child, you may have to accept that you and the family are not suited. You may have to suggest that the parents look for another childcarer with whom they could have a better relationship.

? Learning more

You can learn more about working with parents by taking Unit 4 of the CACHE Diploma in Home-based Childcare.

Confidentiality

Link to ICP
Section 8d

If you are a nanny, you may find that there is a confidentiality clause in your contract, but any professional childcarer should be very vigilant about confidentiality.

As you get to know families, you will acquire a lot of information about them, especially if you are a nanny, living with the family. You will be told some information directly (by parents or other professionals) and some of it you will pick up indirectly (sometimes from the children). Some of this information must be treated in a confidential way.

⚠ Think about it!

Confidentiality means not sharing with other people or passing on personal information about the families you are working with.

Think about what sort of information about families you should be careful with and not pass on.

> My 'never talk about it' list includes parents' relationship difficulties, financial and business matters, and health issues.
>
> **Baz**

> I've always known that it would be unprofessional to tell other people about a lot of a family's personal information, but I only realised recently that even saying where a family live might be risky when a mother and children are escaping domestic violence.
>
> **Carrie**

There are only two sets of circumstances in which you can share or pass on confidential information.

• If parents have given permission for you to do so. For example, you may suggest that it would help if you shared information about a child's progress with a health visitor, but always check with parents that they are happy for you to talk about their child to another professional, and agree what you will say with them.

> My test for deciding what sort of information should remain confidential is to think about how I would feel if such information about me and my family was general knowledge.
>
> **Milly**

- If it is essential to do so in the interests of a child, for example, if you suspect that a child is being abused. (We will look at abuse in Chapter 9.) There may be circumstances when you should – in fact must – pass on information without any previous discussion with the parents, in the interests of protecting children from harm. A child's welfare must always take top priority.

Childminders in particular may find they experience a lot of pressures which make it difficult to keep information confidential. You may find that other people around you – parents of other minded children, your friends, neighbours, your own family, even other childminders – are curious about the children you care for and their families, and try to get you to tell them things that should remain confidential. There have been some high-profile stories of nannies for 'celebrity' families passing on information inappropriately to the media.

Key to good practice

Give some thought to how you will deal with such pressures and enquiries.

✓ Never discuss one set of parents with another.

✓ Take care about casual conversations with friends and family, and at meetings with other childcarers.

✓ Be cautious even in training course sessions and in preparing course work assignments: make references to children and families in a general way and don't refer to them by name.

Alert your own family members that they should be careful about passing on information about the children and families you work with. If you are a childminder, keep written information about children and families securely in a lockable personal record box so no-one in or visiting your home can have access to what you write.

Learning more

You can learn more about confidentiality and data protection by taking Unit 4 of the CACHE Diploma in Home-based Childcare.

Responding to unwanted behaviour

Link to ICP
Sections 5a, 5b and 5d

There will be times when children's behaviour falls short of your expectations. Think about how you are going to respond to behaviour which you don't find acceptable. Start by thinking why the child is behaving in a challenging way.

⚠ Think about it!

Maybe it's because they:

- are at a particular stage in their development so they:
  - are curious and want to explore their environment
  - have no realisation of the danger of a situation
  - are testing limits to see how far adults or other children can be pushed
  - are frustrated that they can't do certain things or communicate their thoughts
  - don't yet have much control over their emotions
  - have a learning difficulty which is hampering the development of their reasoning, communication and other skills
- don't understand adults' explanations of what behaviour is expected

Try to understand children's behaviour

- find adults aren't consistent – they react differently to behaviour from one day to the next – behaviour which was OK yesterday apparently isn't today
- are frightened or anxious (for example, by separation from parents), or unsettled or confused by events in their lives (for example, moving house, having a new childminder or nanny, birth of a sibling, death of a grandparent)
- feel restricted by lack of space to play
- are confused by the way adults behave so they may copy what they *think* others are doing (for example, an adult pulling up plants in the garden)
- have a sensitivity, for example, to food additives which makes them irritable, agitated, unable to concentrate, or even aggressive
- are tired, hungry, bored or sickening for something
- are 'attention seeking' (Why are they not getting attention? Is 'behaving badly' the only way to get it?)
- are not used to a clear and consistent framework for behaviour.

There are various strategies for responding to unwanted behaviour, according to:

- the child's stage of development
- the situation (for example, is there a danger that the child or someone else will get hurt?)
- their previous experiences of adults' response to the way they behave.

> *I find the best way with young children is distraction, I just offer them something more attractive and interesting to do. If they're holding something breakable or dangerous, I replace it with a safe object. If there's danger, I simply stop the child and say 'no' very firmly.*
>
> **Di**

> *One of my main methods is to remove the child from the situation – perhaps to somewhere less interesting for a short while. But I never humiliate or belittle the child by using a 'naughty chair' or shutting them away – I just give them a bit of 'time out' to calm down.*
>
> **Kamini**

> *I think it's important not to reward unacceptable behaviour by giving attention to the child. I turn away and get busy with other children. I try never to argue with the child – I just say a short, sharp 'That's enough,' with a serious expression on my face.*
>
> **Maisie**

> *My approach to tantrums is to restrain the child gently but firmly until the tantrum subsides. If we're in a public place, I try to remove them to somewhere out of view and wait for them to calm down. When they're coming out of it, I give cuddles to soothe and reassure.*
>
> **Kathy**

> *I help them think up alternatives to swear words, like 'spanners'.*
>
> **Gerry**

> *I think it's unfair to label toddlers as 'terrible twos'. It's just that at that age some children get very frustrated because they are developing strong emotions, but they can't yet communicate what they feel and want.*
>
> **Nina**

However you choose to handle challenging behaviour, try to follow a few basic guidelines.

Key to good practice

✓ Make it clear that *you* are in charge. Say no and mean no – and make sure you give the same message by your facial expression and tone of voice.

✓ Show disapproval and make it clear that the behaviour is not acceptable. But if you say something like 'I still love you, but I didn't like what you did', the child will understand it's the behaviour you're rejecting, not them. Don't shame a child by making them sit on a 'naughty step' in view of others.

✓ Explain that what they have done is dangerous, hurtful or unpleasant.

✓ If they have hurt someone else, you may want to insist they say sorry – but remember this depends on how far they understand that being really sorry means 'I wish I hadn't done it, and I won't do it again.'

✓ When an incident is over, always go back to your normal affectionate relationship – show you care about the child – give plenty of cuddles.

Registered childcarers are not permitted by law to slap, smack, bite or shake a child. (It is especially dangerous to shake a child.) But no professional childcarer should consider physical punishment because:

• it is not an effective way of managing children's behaviour. Most young children find it difficult to make a connection between what they have done and the smack they receive, so smacking won't prevent the behaviour happening again

• if you hit a child it simply teaches them that it's OK to be aggressive or unpleasant towards other people.

Parents may say they want you to smack their child, but have a different view from you about what 'smack' is – what is a 'tap' to one person may be a 'blow' to another. They may, after the event, say they didn't mean you could smack that hard, or on that part of the child's body, or for that reason, and accuse you of assaulting their child. Explain to parents that it is not part of your professional care to children to smack them.

Think about it!

Think very carefully about what you will achieve if you decide to punish a child. You might use a sanction like withholding a treat, but this will only work if the punishment or sanction follows the behaviour immediately and the child understands what behaviour the punishment is related to. Remember, the punishment on its own won't explain to the child how you want them to behave in future.

Remember to end each incident with a hug

You need to work closely with parents to achieve continuity and consistency in handling children's behaviour. You may find that some parents expect rules which are different from the ones you usually work with, or have attitudes to punishment that are different from yours. If children face totally different expectations from their parents and from you, it can be very confusing and difficult for them to measure up to what's expected, so you may need to negotiate a compromise with parents. The best situation for the child is one in which you have shared rules and shared strategies.

Key to good practice

If concerns or difficulties arise about children's behaviour, it is essential for you and parents to discuss the matter thoroughly. They may be able to identify something in the child's life which is unsettling them. If you and they feel that efforts need to be made to change the behaviour, you should plan together what to do, and keep each other well informed about how your plans are going.

One potential flashpoint for children's behaviour is at the beginning and end of the day, when children move from the care of their parents to you and back again. This is when the need for you and parents to have a united front about what is and is not expected is most essential – otherwise the children will play you and their parents off against one another.

The overall purpose of the way you manage children's behaviour should be to help them develop self-discipline. As they grow, they need to learn how to control their behaviour for themselves, not always have an adult controlling it for them.

Learning more

You can learn more about managing children's behaviour by taking Unit 2 of the CACHE Diploma in Home-based Childcare.

Children's illness

Nannies are usually expected to continue to provide care for children when they are ill, but childminders should have a firm policy about not caring for a child who has an infectious disease like measles or chickenpox, or a child with vomiting and diarrhoea. The other children in your care, your own family and you are all vulnerable to getting the infection too, and spreading the illness further. It is more difficult for you to provide the proper level of care for an ill child if you have other children to look after, and children who are ill are usually happier in their own homes.

As part of agreeing a contract, I discuss plans for children's illness with parents. I explain where I draw the line in looking after sick children, and check that parents realise that it's likely they will have to take time off work or make other arrangements if the child is ill.

Marian

However, most childminders feel more willing and able to care for children who have the snuffles or a mild cold. Not all employers have 'family-friendly' policies, and many make it very difficult for parents to have time off when their children are ill.

And, of course, children can become unwell at any time when they're in your care, so you need to be prepared to deal with the situation.

Giving medication requires the written permission of parents

Key to good practice

✓ Have parents' contact details readily at hand. Sometimes you may need to ask the parent to come urgently, but often you will just let them know about the child's symptoms and, if you're a childminder, the need to be prompt in collecting the child.

✓ You should never give any form of medication without the written instructions of a parent. You may not know about a child's allergies or possible adverse reaction to medication.

✓ If you have written instructions to give medication, make sure you:

- keep it stored safely out of reach of the children

- give the doses in the amounts and at the times set out in the instructions

- make a note each time you give a dose of the amount and time, and get parents to sign your record to show they have seen it.

✓ If you are a childminder and one of the minded children or your own children contracts an infectious disease, make sure you tell the parents of other minded children because it's quite likely that their child will catch it.

Learning more

You can learn more about dealing with children's illness by taking Unit 2 of the CACHE Diploma in Home-based Childcare.

CHAPTER 9

When the going gets tough

This chapter will help and guide you through potentially difficult situations, such as bullying and disagreements with parents.

9 When the going gets tough

There will be times in your work as a home-based childcarer when you come up against difficult situations which will challenge your skills and personal resources. This chapter looks at:

- bullying
- disagreements with parents
- protecting children from abuse
- concerns about children's development
- seeking support to help you get through these and other times when you find your work is making demands on you.

Bullying

A child you care for may be being bullied – or may be bullying other children. Bullying is most common in school-age children, though it can begin in younger children. The bullying may be happening at school, or on the journey to and from school.

Link to ICP
Section 7e

⚠ Think about it!

It is important that adults intervene to prevent and stop bullying because it can be serious and have very damaging effects. Children who are bullied often become very unhappy: bullying undermines their self-esteem and confidence, leading to anxiety or even depression. It also damages children who bully: some children who bully remain bullies all their lives towards other members of their family or at work.

What is bullying?

Bullying is about exercising power over another person in a negative and hurtful way. It takes many forms, such as:

- physical attack – punching, slapping, kicking, pushing, poking; damaging belongings
- verbal attack – teasing about appearance, ethnicity, disability or sexual orientation; taunting about family or friends; threats; spreading rumours
- exclusion – from activities, the group; ridiculing, humiliating
- extortion – demanding money or possessions with threats of physical attack.

Girls as well as boys bully, though in different ways – girls tend to use less physical aggression, but more verbal and social pressure like teasing or exclusion. And girls may bully boys as well as vice versa.

One form of bullying is exclusion

What makes bullying different from incidents of aggressive behaviour is that it consists of persistent attempts to cause pain and distress. The bully gains satisfaction from their ability to manipulate and intimidate others.

Why do children bully?

There are many possible explanations of why children become bullies, such as:

- they have learned to behave in aggressive ways because they experience violence at home
- they are not able to feel with or for other people (empathise), so they don't realise how much their behaviour hurts other people
- either they lack communication and social skills, so they lash out at others; or they have effective social skills, but use them to dominate or exclude others
- they are not secure in their own emotional development and feel weak, but they feel superior when they hurt other people – they want to exercise power over others as a way of making them feel better about themselves. Some people get a 'hit' from seeing others unhappy and put in a weak position, so they do it again and again to maintain their own insecure feelings.

Think about it!

It is sometimes said that some children almost seem to invite bullying. It is true that some children who are 'different' – in skin colour, disability, appearance, the way they speak or dress – are especially vulnerable to bullying, and some children with low self-esteem feel that they don't deserve to be treated well. But we must beware of blaming the bullied child – they have a right to have their 'difference' respected and to be protected from bullies.

Responding to bullying

You can help prevent bullying by supporting children who are bullied and playing a part in tackling the emotional development and behaviour of the bully.

Key to good practice

If a child you care for tells you they are being bullied:

✓ never ignore it, take what they say seriously and acknowledge that they are angry or frightened about what has happened

✓ reassure them that you'll do all you can to help, praise them for telling and say it's not their fault

✓ keep a record of the incidents the child tells you about

✓ talk to the child's parents, and approach the school together

✓ help the child to build their self-esteem and self-confidence.

You can help a child who has been bullied to understand that it's best to:

• walk away when the bully appears: tell them that it's sensible, not cowardly

• not fight back: that can make things worse

• 'walk tall' – stand up straight, walk confidently, shoulders back, make eye contact (you and they could practise with a mirror)

• be with other children in a group as much as possible, not on your own

• react as little as possible – don't reward the bully with responding (you could practise this through stories with puppets or dolls).

Key to good practice

If you discover that a child you care for is a bully:

- ✓ explain why the behaviour is not acceptable, help them to see the consequences of their actions and how it hurts other people
- ✓ talk with their parents
- ✓ help to find acceptable ways of the child expressing their own strength and building their self-esteem.

Bullying can only flourish under a code of silence and out-dated ideas that it's 'wrong to tell tales'. Always make it clear that bullying will not be tolerated and that children who experience or witness bullying must tell – and then, most importantly, you and other adults must respond and take positive action.

Preventing bullying

There are several ways of preventing bullying.

Key to good practice

You can help to prevent the children you care for becoming bullies or getting bullied by:

- ✓ encouraging positive behaviour by making clear what behaviour is and is not tolerated, praising for good behaviour, and pointing out hurtful behaviour
- ✓ promoting respect for each individual – helping children to learn that everyone is special, and that we must value and respect other people, including those who are different from ourselves
- ✓ building children's trust in you so they can tell you about what is worrying, upsetting or hurting them – showing that you listen to them, and letting them know that you take what they say seriously
- ✓ building children's self-esteem by helping them to feel good about themselves, and to know that they are valued – this will help both the bullied and the bullies.

? Learning more

You can learn more about helping children to protect themselves against bullying by taking Unit 3 of the CACHE Diploma in Home-based Childcare.

Kidscape publish booklets which you can get via their website www.kidscape.org.uk or by sending a large SAE with six stamps to the Kidscape head office (see the Useful contacts section at the back of this book).

Organisations like Kidscape publish information about how to deal with bullying

Disagreements with parents

Link to ICP
Section 4f

Most of the time you will get on well with the parents of the children you care for, but there may be times when relationships with some parents become less positive. You may go on being polite to one another, but for some reason, you feel less warm towards one another. Children get upset by difficulties in relationships between the most significant people in their lives, even if they don't really understand all of what is going on, so it is important to tackle such problems and not let the situation drag on.

Do your best to be professional and try to understand things from the parents' point of view. They have strong emotions about their children which may make them less objective about some situations.

> *My golden rule is to raise any problems or concerns with a parent at an early stage. I've learned this from experience. There was one situation where I got more and more resentful and frustrated about the way I felt the parents were treating me, to the point where I just couldn't communicate with them calmly any more. It all turned out to be a big misunderstanding, but the whole thing nearly led to a breakdown in the nannying arrangements. I've also learned that if parents seem to be irritated or annoyed with me, I don't have to wait for them to be the first to raise the subject. It's better to clear the air and discuss everything honestly.*
>
> **Ginny**

Key to good practice

If you find yourself in a strained relationship with parents, try following these guidelines.

- ✓ Arrange a time to talk when the children are not around and needing your attention.
- ✓ Make a note of the main things you want to say.
- ✓ Try to remain calm and pleasant; don't shout.
- ✓ Explain the situation as you see it – stick to the facts and be brief, but bring all the issues into the open.
- ✓ Don't make accusations.
- ✓ Explain how the situation is affecting you and how you feel.
- ✓ Listen to the response carefully and without interrupting, and try to appreciate how the other person is feeling and sees things.
- ✓ Focus on the areas where you both agree and look for a compromise; stick to the most important issues and don't get sidelined by details.
- ✓ Clarify what you have decided together, perhaps put it in writing to avoid further misunderstanding.

> *Some parents can be really fussy about every little detail, and others seem to be reluctant to spend much time talking to me about their children. Either can be infuriating, but I try to understand what's going on. Maybe it's because they feel guilty that they don't spend much time with the children, or they're under a lot of pressure at work. Sometimes you have to be very patient and understanding, and make a lot of allowances.*
>
> Pat

Clear the air with an honest discussion

Complaints

You may find yourself in a situation where a parent makes a complaint about your service. If you have drawn up a simple complaints procedure which you shared with parents, they will know how to tell you about their concerns, and you will be able to follow your procedure for considering the complaint and responding in a professional way.

Occasionally, parents complain to the regulating authority. If this happens to you, make sure you keep copies of any letters.

Learning more

You can learn more about dealing with conflicts and communication difficulties, and protecting yourself against complaints by taking Unit 4 of the CACHE Diploma in Home-based Childcare.

The most common disagreements between parents and childminders are contract disputes. NCMA publishes a briefing sheet which you can get by contacting their information line on 0800 169 4486.

Protecting children from abuse

Link to ICP
Section 7c

It is very important that you are well-informed about child abuse since, like all childcare professionals, you might find yourself in contact with an abused child. Don't think that it could never happen to you because you work with 'nice families'. Child abuse happens in all social and cultural groups in our society. Besides being aware of some of the signs of abuse, you must know what to do if you are concerned.

Note: If reading and thinking about this topic raises painful and difficult issues about your own childhood, or you find it shocking or painful, you might want to contact Childwatch (see the Useful contacts section at the back of this book).

Think about it!

Children, especially young children, are very vulnerable and cannot seek help for themselves. They rely on adults to protect them from pain and distress.

Abuse can have long lasting traumatic effects which may damage children's development, both physical and emotional. Children who have been abused may grow up feeling they are worthless and find difficulty in forming happy relationships, or even become abusers themselves.

It's estimated that 150–200 children die in England and Wales every year as the result of abuse or neglect – that's three or four a week. Children of all ages, from tiny babies to teenagers, including disabled children, are abused.

Children are more likely to be abused by people they know (including members of their own family) than by strangers.

Forms of child abuse

The main forms of child abuse are:

Link to ICP
Section 7a

- physical
- sexual
- emotional
- neglect.

Physical abuse consists of someone deliberately inflicting a physical injury on a child by hitting, shaking, squeezing, burning (sometimes with cigarettes), biting, giving them poisonous or harmful substances (such as drugs or alcohol).

Physical abuse can cause bruises, burns, fractures, internal injuries, brain damage – even death.

Sexual abuse consists of an adult using a child to meet their own sexual needs. This may range from showing pornographic magazines or videos, or fondling through to masturbation, oral sex or intercourse.

Sexual abuse can have damaging, long lasting emotional effects including having difficulty in later life in forming trusting and stable personal relationships.

Emotional abuse consists of continually failing to show love or affection to a child, severe and persistent rejection, criticising, harassment, taunting, ridiculing, belittling, frightening, threatening – and also bullying (which is sometimes listed as a separate form of abuse).

Neglect can lead to mental and physical health problems

Emotional abuse can cause a child to become nervous, withdrawn, lacking in confidence and self-esteem, or aggressive.

Neglect consists of persistent or severe failure to meet a child's basic physical needs to the point where their health and development are adversely affected, by exposing a child to cold, not providing adequate food, not ensuring basic cleanliness and hygiene, leaving them unattended, failing to seek medical attention.

Neglect can lead to a child 'failing to thrive' and having health problems.

Possible signs of abuse

Link to ICP
Section 7b

An older child may actually tell you that someone is upsetting or hurting them. However, younger children may not have the communication skills to explain to you what is happening, so you need to be aware of a range of possible signs of abuse.

If you see these physical signs, a child may be being abused:

- bruises or cuts, particularly on parts of the body which are not normally injured in accidents (the back, back of legs, buttocks, eyes, ears, cheeks, mouth and neck, upper/inner arms, stomach, chest, genital and rectal areas)

- bruises of different shades from dark blue/purple to yellowing – these are likely to be of varying ages and indicate that a child has received the injuries over a period of time

- burns – especially small round burns which could have been caused by a cigarette

- loss of weight, eating problems (over-eating, loss of appetite)

- inappropriately dressed, or dirty, or smelly child

- irritation in the genital area.

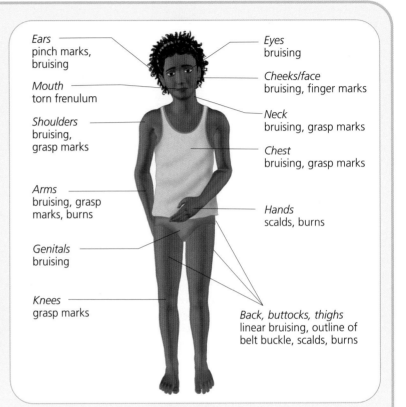

Ears
pinch marks, bruising

Mouth
torn frenulum

Shoulders
bruising, grasp marks

Arms
bruising, grasp marks, burns

Genitals
bruising

Knees
grasp marks

Eyes
bruising

Cheeks/face
bruising, finger marks

Neck
bruising, grasp marks

Chest
bruising, grasp marks

Hands
scalds, burns

Back, buttocks, thighs
linear bruising, outline of belt buckle, scalds, burns

Usual positions of injuries in cases of child abuse

It might point to possible abuse if a child:

- behaves in a sexually explicit way (for example, playing games and showing awareness of sexual matters inappropriate for the child's age)

- only seems happy when they're with you

- doesn't trust adults or watches adults fearfully

- has disturbed sleep or nightmares, or wets the bed

- inflicts wounds on themselves or makes suicide attempts

- reverts to younger behaviour

- is withdrawn or depressed

- begins to behave in a different way such as suddenly becoming very quiet or developing aggressive behaviour or severe tantrums.

These are possible signs, but many of them may have other explanations. For instance, a certain kind of rash can make a child look as though their face has been slapped, and some birthmarks can look like bruises. Changes in behaviour can have many explanations. You should not rush into making an assumption that a child has been abused but, if you observe several of these signs, or they are persistent or extreme, alarm bells should be set off for you.

What to do if you think a child is being abused

Link to ICP
Section 7f

▷ Take action!

Your local authority should provide you with written information about the procedures you should follow if you suspect abuse. If you do not have a copy, contact your local social services department or Children's Information Service.

🔍 Key to good practice

If you are concerned that a child may be being abused, you should:

✓ contact your local social services department

✓ write down what you've seen and observed, with dates and times. Stick to hard factual information – don't include your interpretation of the situation or your theories about what has happened. A good way to approach recording information is to think of your senses (sight, hearing, etc.)

  • I heard (her say…, his mum shout…) – using their exact words, and also write down what you said to the child
  • I saw (the children came to my house in the winter rain wearing only thin summer dresses)
  • I felt (his hands were very cold)
  • I smelled (stale urine on her clothes).

✓ be aware of confidentiality – make sure you keep these notes where no-one else can see them, and don't discuss the matter with family or friends, only with other relevant professionals such as social workers

▶

Record what you have observed

✔ inform your regulatory body, such as Ofsted or CSIW, of the action you have taken

✔ keep your focus on the care of the child, giving warm, calm comfort and reassurance.

If a child starts to tell you about any harm they are experiencing, listen carefully to what they tell you, but don't push them to say more: allow them to communicate in their own way and at their own pace. Explain to them that you have to share the information with other people to try to help them.

In some circumstances, you might seek an explanation for an injury or sudden change in behaviour from the parents. But don't do this if a child has told you that it is a parent who is harming them.

Deciding whether to take action

If you suspect that a child is being abused, you must take action – don't ignore the situation.

It is not your role to investigate suspected abuse, but you have a duty to report your concerns and protect the child. You may feel uncertain about whether to do this, but keep in mind your responsibility to the child and put their welfare first.

You could prevent a child suffering – or even save their life.

The usual policy of social services departments is to try to keep families together, rather than taking children into local authority care and separating them from the rest of the family. Their aim is to help and advise the family to ensure the child is safe in future. It is only in extreme cases, where children are at great risk, that a family is broken up, or there is a criminal prosecution.

> *I had some suspicions but I couldn't believe that an adult, someone I knew, who was related to the child, could deliberately harm a child.*
>
> **Elaine**

> *I was afraid that the family would be split up and the children taken away.*
>
> **Hasina**

Spotlight on practice

Natasha is a nanny, and she became very concerned about one of the children she cared for, but she was unsure whether or not to take action and report the situation to social services. She contacted NCMA and was put in touch with an NCMA member of staff. She was very relieved to get advice and help with thinking through the seriousness of her concerns. She was given a lot of support and information about what to do next.

Spotlight on practice

Paul is a childminder and was in a similar situation. He contacted the NSPCC and was also given a lot of help and support to take the matter forward.

Helping children to protect themselves

Most children are naturally trusting of adults and, sadly, there are some adults who will take advantage of this trust. Children need to learn how to protect themselves from abuse, just as they need to learn how to avoid other dangers in life such as traffic and fire. You can play a part in this by helping them to understand ideas like:

Link to ICP
Section 7d

- you have a right to say no if someone tries to touch you or make you do something which frightens you or you don't like: your body belongs to you and you can choose who you want to hold, hug, cuddle or kiss you

- if someone has done something to you that you didn't like, and asks you to keep it secret, that is a 'bad secret' and you don't have to keep it – tell another adult you know you can trust

- you should never go to someone's house – not even someone you know well - without first asking your parents or your childcarer

- if you are out without adults, you should not talk to or go with someone you don't know. (But don't put too much emphasis on 'stranger danger' – remember that most children are abused by adults they know.)

Above all, build children's self-esteem and self-confidence. Children who value themselves and are sure of their own worth are less likely to be abused or bullied. Children who have low self-esteem are more likely to be vulnerable to abuse.

Building children's self-esteem will help them to protect themselves

Link to ICP
Section 7g

Learning more

A source of useful information on helping children to learn how to protect themselves is provided by the organisation, Kidscape.

Allegations against childcarers

From time to time, nannies, childminders and members of childminders' families are accused of abusing children. The teenage sons of childminders are especially vulnerable to this sort of accusation. Sometimes parents make such allegations because they are trying to cover up their own abuse of children.

You need to be aware that you are vulnerable to such allegations because you work alone in your own or a family's home. Protect yourself and your family by:

• keeping records of accidents and also of incidents such as a child arriving at your house with signs of an injury. Ask parents to sign your record to show that they accept what has happened or what you have noticed

• encouraging children to manage as much of their own personal care as possible – this helps children build their skills and confidence, and also reduces your vulnerability to allegations.

This doesn't mean that you should feel nervous and inhibited about touching children. There are times when a child needs comfort and reassurance, and an important part of this is a hug. Physical touch is an essential part of communicating with young children, and if you did not show affection towards the children you care for, you would be neglecting their emotional welfare.

If an allegation is made against a home-based childcarer, an investigation must be carried out. If such a thing ever happens to you, NCMA can offer you information about possible courses of action open to you.

Learning more

NCMA has a valuable publication, *Safeguarding children*.

You can learn more about child protection by taking Unit 3 of the CACHE Diploma in Home-based Childcare.

Concerns about children's development

Link to ICP
Section 8b

As you get to know a child, you may become concerned that they are not progressing as you might have expected. You may observe that they are not reaching the 'developmental milestones' for a child of their age. Of course, you should remember that the range of 'normal' development is very broad. For example, some children don't walk until they are nearly two, or talk much until they are past their second birthday – but you would be right to feel that this was worrying in a child of nearly three.

You can play an important role in the family's life by explaining sympathetically why you think things aren't quite right, and help them seek advice from their health visitor or GP. The earlier potential signs of disability or learning difficulties are spotted, the more that can be done to help the child.

You need to be very sensitive in the way you share your concerns with parents. Sometimes parents are reluctant to recognise that their child's development is delayed. On the other hand, you may find that they are already quite worried, and will appreciate your opinion and reassurance.

If you feel you need advice about a child's progress and how to raise the matter with parents, contact your local area Special Educational Needs Co-ordinator (SENCO). The Children's Information Service should be able to help you make contact.

Explain your concerns to parents in a sensitive way

Learning more

You can learn more about working with disabled children by taking Unit 2 of the CACHE Diploma in Home-based Childcare.

Seeking support

Link to ICP
Section 8j

If you encounter any of the situations we have looked at in this chapter, you are likely to need some support, advice and help to deal with it. Home-based childcare can be a lonely job. You don't have colleagues readily at hand in your workplace to talk over concerns, or seek advice and information.

Sometimes people think that seeking support is a sign of weakness, but it is not. It requires strength and maturity, and is the professional way. Getting support, rather than struggling on alone, makes you more effective in your work.

Take action!

As a professional childcarer, you need to begin to build up links with other professionals such as:

* NCMA, SCMA or NICMA development workers
* local authority early years advisers
* health visitors
* teachers.

Gather together information about relevant people in your area and take up any opportunities to meet significant people like this. If you already know people, it is much easier to turn to them for advice and support when you need it.

Remember that if you seek advice about a child, you should not pass on confidential information unless you have discussed your concerns with parents first and obtained their permission (except when a child protection issue is involved).

Childminding groups offer support

Childminding groups can provide mutual support and give opportunities to talk through uncertainties and difficulties. Sharing experiences can help you cope. It's a comfort to know that someone else has faced similar circumstances; it helps prevent problems getting out of proportion. You must be careful to guard confidentiality, and not talk about families by name.

Most people turn initially for personal support to their family, friends or neighbours. You may find this helps you to sort out your feelings about a situation, give you confidence to face your difficulties, and encourage you to carry on when you feel low. But if you seek support from such personal sources, it can be difficult to maintain professional confidentiality and not pass on personal details of the families you work with.

Spotlight on practice

Bella is a childminder. She was concerned that one of the minded children might have a hearing impairment. She had mentioned it to the parents but they seemed uncertain. Fortunately, she had made a note of the details of a speech and language therapist who had recently come along to the local childminding group one evening to talk about child development concerns so she was able to make contact and get useful advice.

Spotlight on practice

Jessie is a nanny. One of the children had a rash and earache. Neither she nor the parents knew whether these symptoms might be serious, but she had developed a good relationship with the family's health visitor already so she felt confident in seeking advice promptly.

Seek advice and information when you need support

Spotlight on practice

Kirsty is a childminder who reported concerns about a child to social services which led to an investigation. She was shocked, angry and revolted by what she had discovered. She was also asked to come to a case conference and warned that in due course she might be asked to appear in court as a witness, and she felt anxious about this.

She had met the local NCMA development worker, Steve, at several events, and made contact with him right away. Steve spent a lot of time helping her to talk about how she felt. He helped her prepare for the case conference by explaining what would happen, who else would be involved, and the role Kirsty was expected to play. He reassured her that if she did have to go to court, he would come along too.

Kirsty knew that Steve understood the confidentiality issues involved and could be trusted to act in a professional way.

You may feel a little nervous at first about approaching professionals like these, but there is a growing awareness of the need for people who work with children to co-operate and work as a team to ensure the well-being and safety of children. All professionals are developing their understanding of 'multi-agency' work, and see the benefits of professionals from different organisations and in different roles all working together. Be confident about your own professional role, and remember that you know the children you work with extremely well – better than other professionals are likely to and that makes you worth listening to!

? Learning more

You can learn more about working with other professionals by taking Unit 3 of the CACHE Diploma in Home-based Childcare.

CHAPTER 10

The future

This chapter will help you think about the future and possible career paths open to you.

10 The future

As you settle into your job as a home-based childcarer, you can begin to think about what it could lead to for you in the future. This chapter looks at:

- training and qualifications
- quality assurance
- career pathways.

Training and qualifications

Link to ICP
Section 8k

When you started your job as a home-based childcarer, you brought knowledge and skills to the work, based on your past learning about working with children and families, and your previous experience. In order to be registered as a childminder or approved as a home childcarer, you will have learned more about home-based childcare through your introductory training.

Now you are settling into your new role, it is important for you to think about how you can keep your development as a professional going. A professional never feels that they 'know it all' or are 'fully qualified': they know that there is so much to continue to learn about their job – new developments, new ideas, new approaches. This is especially important in a job as skilled and demanding as looking after other people's children.

One essential way to develop yourself professionally is to seek out and grasp opportunities for further training. Don't be put off by thinking that training courses will be like school – sitting formally behind a desk and having to write essays. You will find that they are informal and friendly, with lots of opportunities to discuss ideas and share experiences. Some childcarers become addicted to training once they have had a taste of it!

▶ Take action!

Find out about relevant training available in your area.

- Your local Children's Information Service should be able to tell you about one-off workshops or short courses offered by, for example, the Early Years Development and Childcare Partnership.
- Colleges can tell you about longer courses, or you can contact NCMA, SCMA or NICMA.

Find out too about distance learning offered by, for example, the National Extension College (see the Useful contacts section at the back of this book).

When you're deciding what training to pursue, there are a number of questions to ask.

- Will this training be recognised in other parts of the country? If you do training which is only recognised in the area you live in now, it may not be acknowledged if you move to another area. Check that it is part of a national framework.

- Will the training lead to a qualification and, if so, what will you have to do to gain the qualification – sit an exam or write assignments, or be assessed in some other way?
- Is the qualification at least Level 3 and so suitable for people who work on their own? (Level 2 is only suitable for people who work under the supervision of others, so home-based childcarers should aim to achieve a Level 3 qualification.)
- Are the training sessions held in a place and at times which are convenient for you?
- How can you get help with the cost?

NCMA, SCMA and NICMA can help you get the answers to questions like this.

Spotlight on practice

Rhona is a childminder. When she registered, she completed the ICP course (Introduction to Childcare Practice – home-based) and she passed the test of multiple choice questions. Recently, she went to a local childminding conference and got talking to an NCMA development worker, Chris, who explained to her that this means that she already had Unit 1 of the Diploma in Home-based Childcare (DHC), a qualification awarded by CACHE (Council for Awards in Children's Care and Education), and recognised throughout England and Wales. Rhona found out that there are four other units in the DHC:

- Unit 2 Childcare and child development
- Unit 3 The childcare practitioner in the home-based setting
- Unit 4 Working in partnership with parents in the home-based setting
- Unit 5 Planning to meet children's individual learning needs in the home-based setting.

Each of the courses is 30 hours long and Chris said that Rhona could take the units in any order. Rhona was pleased that the sessions were held in the evenings, giving her time to get to the community centre where they were held after the children she minded had gone home. There is an assignment to do to get the unit, but Chris reassured Rhona that she would get lots of guidance and support to complete it. Chris helped Rhona get funding and sent her information on how to enrol.

Rhona decided that she wanted to be a qualified childminder to show parents how committed she is to the job. It's many years since she did any studying and she realised that it would take a lot of time and hard work, but she thought it all looked very interesting and would help her to do her job to the very best of her ability.

She is finding the tutor (who used to be a childminder herself) very friendly and approachable, and the sessions aren't at all like school. There is a lot of discussion and sharing ideas and experiences. She is enjoying meeting the other childminders on the course and having the chance to think seriously about all that is involved in her responsible role.

Training is enjoyable (©NCMA)

Spotlight on practice

Rachel is a nanny. She did the CACHE Certificate in Child Care and Education when she was at school, and has attended quite a number of workshops and short courses. She has decided that she now wants to gain a qualification which will be relevant to working on her own. When she enquired at the local college, it was explained that she should aim for a Level 3 qualification, and her best option would be a National Vocational Qualification (NVQ) in Children's Care, Learning and Development (CCLD).

The college runs regular workshop sessions which will help Rachel extend her knowledge and skills. There are some compulsory (mandatory) units, but she will be able to choose from a long list of optional units. She will be assessed through observation and other methods which show 'evidence' of how she does her current job.

Rachel explained what she wanted to do to the parents who employ her and she was delighted that they were very supportive of her aims to improve her qualifications. They have given their permission for the NVQ assessor to come into their home to observe Rachel working with their children, and agreed to provide information to the assessor about the quality of her work, for example, in handling the children's behaviour.

Spotlight on practice

Sian is a childminder who lives in a very rural area. When she enquired from NCMA Wales about DHC courses, they told her that there were so few childminders in her area, a course was not viable. However, they sent her information about the DHC courses offered by the National Extension College.

Sian is finding this a very flexible way to learn, as she can do the work at any time and at her own pace, fitting it in round her childminding and her family life. Her tutor is available by phone and has helped her when she has got stuck or didn't quite understand something.

Spotlight on practice

Liz is a childminder. She completed the CACHE Certificate in Childminding Practice a few years ago, and also gained an NVQ at Level 3. She really got the learning bug and wanted to go on to a higher qualification. She came across a leaflet in a magazine which gave details of The Open University's Early Years Foundation Degree. She managed to get some funding from her local authority, and enrolled on the course. She has been finding it really stretches her, but she was delighted to find that the OU materials talk about childminding situations as well as those in groups. She likes the way it is related to the reality of her everyday work as well as giving her the chance to learn some of the theories about how children develop and learn.

Always see training as an opportunity, and take advantage of any that you can find time and energy for. It will renew and refresh you in your work, and make you feel increasingly confident.

Quality assurance

Think about your professional development as a journey, which goes on throughout your career in working with children and families. It is not only about going on training courses and gaining

Link to ICP
Section 8k

qualifications, or about reaching a point where you feel you know and can do everything that the job requires. In recent years, the idea of quality assurance has helped us to see that a professional worker needs to take time regularly to:

* think about how they work and why they work the way they do (reflect on practice)
* identify the aspects of their job that they do well and effectively, and the aspects where they feel less secure and realise their performance could be improved
* plan how they can expand their knowledge and develop their skills so they are able to tackle the aspects of work they find more challenging.

In some areas, the local authority has its own quality assurance programme but there are two schemes developed by NCMA. They are specifically geared to the needs of home-based childcarers, recognised throughout England and Wales, and have been endorsed by the government through Investors in Children.

Children Come First is a scheme for approving childminding networks. In a formal childminding network, a co-ordinator is employed to visit childminders, check that their practice reaches high standards of quality, provide advice and support, and guide them into appropriate training.

> *Our network co-ordinator, Rosemary, is a fount of knowledge and can always help sort out a tricky situation. I was quite nervous about the idea of having someone come into my home and judge whether I met the NCMA Children Come First Quality Standard, but I need not have worried. Rosemary is so friendly and positive. She always emphasises what she can see I'm doing well – but she's also honest about helping me see where I could be even better. She has helped me get on a course to learn Makaton so I can communicate with a child I care for who has learning difficulties, and the toy library has been a real boon. The meetings of the network childminders are great; we have some really good discussions – and our 'childminders' night out' is always a smash hit!*
>
> **Lynn**

Quality First is a scheme for individual home-based childcarers. It consists of a portfolio of 'reflective practitioner materials' designed to be completed in sections, working at your own pace. Support is available by telephone from a mentor, and you will be visited by an assessor who will want to see you working with the children.

> *I really enjoyed working on the Quality First materials. They made me think about how I work and I found writing down descriptions of my practice gave me confidence that I was doing a good job. It also made me think about things I'd never considered before, and I feel I've improved the way I work. I felt ten feet tall when I got my certificate, and I make sure I put the Quality First logo really prominently on my vacancy ad. And it was such a help in getting ready for my inspection – the inspector was very impressed by my portfolio.*
>
> **Suraya**

NCMA's Quality First is for individual childminders

Taking part in quality assurance is a way of showing parents that you take a professional approach to your work, always aiming to improve the high quality of your service and build on your existing skills.

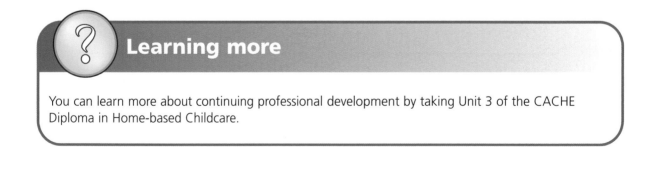

? Learning more

You can learn more about continuing professional development by taking Unit 3 of the CACHE Diploma in Home-based Childcare.

Your career

As we said in the introduction to this book, being a childminder or nanny is a rewarding job, and many people find great satisfaction from remaining in the job for many years. Home-based childcare offers opportunities to expand the way you work into new and interesting roles, providing you with challenges in life and broadening your horizons. You may in due course move on from home-based childcare, perhaps into some other way of working with children and families, but there are a growing number of opportunities to build on your work as a childminder or nanny and get into fascinating new areas of work.

Spotlight on practice

Neil is a member of a childminding network and has become a community childminder. Over the past three years, he has worked with several disabled children, and with children whose families are under a lot of stress, such as the one where the mother had mental health problems. He has also worked with children who have been abused. The additional training he has been able to take part in through the network has helped him develop a wide range of new skills to be able to cope with this very demanding work. Recently, the network has been approached to help some teenage parents, and Neil is discussing with the co-ordinator how he could support some of the young fathers.

Spotlight on practice

Carole is a member of a Children Come First approved childminding network. She has become an accredited childminder. This means she is seen as an 'educator', supporting three four-year-olds in the Foundation Stage of the curriculum. She can offer an additional service to parents who want their children to remain in a home-based setting rather than going into group provision, and her local authority pays her a 'nursery education grant' for doing this work. She has really enjoyed the extra training she has had to be able to do this and she has had a lot of support from the early years teacher attached to the network.

Spotlight on practice

Shirley has become a support childminder. She helps newly-registered childminders and people going through registration, giving them information and advice about their new job, helping them fill in forms, introducing them to the local childminding groups and helping them find training courses. The work fits in very well with her own childminding, and she finds it very satisfying. She enjoys meeting up with other support childminders and the scheme's co-ordinator to compare experiences.

One option for career development is becoming a tutor (©NCMA)

Spotlight on practice

Barbara has become a tutor, delivering courses for the units of the DHC. She has worked for both NCMA and one of the local colleges, and has had the chance to take a qualification in teaching adults, and also some NCMA training on supporting childminders in their learning. She still does some childminding, but has scaled it down as her earnings from tutoring have expanded. When the first batch of 'her' students got their certificates, she was so proud of them and they presented her with a wonderful bouquet.

Spotlight on practice

Wendy had decided that she wanted to move on from being a childminder but she didn't want to leave childminding. When she saw the post for a network co-ordinator and NCMA development worker advertised, she decided to find out more about it, and talked it over with several friends. She found the interview process nerve-wracking as it was many years since she had applied for a job, but when she was offered the post, she knew she had made the right decision. She loves the job and all the new perspectives it gives her.

Whether you decide to develop your career in ways like this, or continue to work as a childminder or nanny, you will always know that you have played a major part in the upbringing of the children you work with, and have contributed to the life of their families.

Useful contacts

Care Standards Inspectorate for Wales (CSIW)
4/5 Charnwood Court
Heol Billingsley
Parc Nantgarw
Nantgarw CF15 7QZ
01443 848450
www.csiw.wales.gov.uk

Child Accident Prevention Trust (CAPT)
Cloister Court
22–26 Farringdon Lane
London EC1R 3AJ
020 7608 3828
www.capt.org.uk

Childcare Approval Scheme
2nd Floor
23–25 Westbury House
Bridge Street
Pinner HA5 3HR
0845 767 8111
www.childcareapprovalscheme.co.uk

Children's Information Service (CIS)
www.childcarecareers.gov.uk
Local contacts link, providing information about
    your nearest CIS

Childwatch
19 Spring Bank
Hull
East Yorkshire HU3 1AF
01482 325 552 (helpline)
www.childwatch.org.uk

Council or Awards in Children's Care and
    Education (CACHE)
Beaufort House
Grosvenor Road
St. Albans
Hertfordshire AL1 3AW
01727 818616
www.cache.org.uk

Criminal Records Bureau (CRB)
CRB Customer Services
PO Box 110
Liverpool L69 3EF
0870 90 90 811
www.crb.gov.uk

HM Revenue and Customs
0845 915 4415 (self-assessment helpline)
0845 915 4655 (National Insurance self-employed
    helpline)
0845 300 3900 (tax credits helpline)
www.hmrc.gov.uk

Kidscape
2 Grosvenor Gardens
London SW1H 0DH
020 7730 3300 (helpline for parents and carers)
08451 205 204 (helpline)
www.kidscape.org.uk

National Childminding Association (NCMA)
Royal Court
81 Tweedy Road
Bromley
Kent BR1 1TG
0845 880 0044
0800 169 4486 (information helpline)
www.ncma.org.uk

National Extension College (NEC)
The Michael Young Centre
Purbeck Road
Cambridge CB2 2HN
01223 400200
www.nec.ac.uk.

National Society for Prevention of Cruelty
    to Children (NSPCC)
Weston House
42 Curtain Road
London EC2A 3NH
0808 800 5000 (helpline)
www.nspcc.org.uk

Northern Ireland Childminding Association
  (NICMA)
16/18 Mill Street
Newtownards
Co. Down BT23 4LU
028 9181 1015
www.nicma.org

Office for Standards in Education (Ofsted)
Alexandra House
33 Kingsway
London WC2B 6SE
020 7421 6800
www.ofsted.gov.uk

Recruitment and Employment Confederation
020 7462 3260
www.rec.uk.com/sector-groups/childcare

Red Cross
UK Office
44 Moorfields
London EC2Y 9AL
0870 170 7000
www.redcross.org.uk

St. John Ambulance
27 St. John's Lane
London EC1M 4BU
08700 10 49 50
www.sja.org.uk

Scottish Childminding Association (SCMA)
Suite 3
7 Melville Terrace
Stirling FK8 2ND
01786 445377
www.childminding.org

Scottish Commission for the Regulation of Care
The Care Commission
Compass House
11 Riverside Drive
Dundee DD1 4NY
www.carecommission.com

Index